IN PRAISE OF *DEAR ABISHAG: LETTERS TO LITTLE-KNOWN WOMEN OF THE BIBLE*

"Roberta Damon has produced another 'must read' book! Using a similar style, she has written an interesting sequel to her recent book, Dear Mrs. Noah: Letters to *...* Bible. *This time, she addresses ... the Bible. Roberta's many years ... and biblical scholar enable her t... and share her insights with her r...*

Dr. Charles Chandler
Founder and Retired Director
of Ministering to Ministers

"They weren't just 'extras' in a story on the pages of our Bibles: They were real people who lived during difficult times and who struggled and loved and knew pain and injustice. Biblical accounts all but overlook them, but God knew them and included their stories and their names in His story."

Beverly Lipford Carroll
Author of *God Chooses People Like You and He Wants You to Know*

"Roberta Damon has done it again! Writing for today's reader, she brings to life thirty obscure biblical women through brief letters. She makes Bible study appealing and includes questions to stimulate thought and discussion."

Fred Anderson
Executive Director Emeritus
Center for Baptist Heritage and Studies and
The Virginia Baptist Historical Society

"Roberta Damon is passionate about expanding the repertoire of biblical witnesses to serve as guides and mentors for her readers in their own faith journey."

Dr. Phyllis Rodgerson Pleasants Tessieri
John F. Loftis Professor of Church History (retired),
Baptist Theological Seminary at Richmond

Dear Abishag: Letters to Little Known WOmen of the Bible

By Roberta M. Damon

HigherLife Development Services, Inc.
PO Box 623307
Oviedo, Florida 32762
(407) 563-4806

www.ahigherlife.com

Printed in the United States of America

10 9 8 7 6 5 4 3 2

Library of Congress Cataloging-in-Publication Data

Print: 978-1-7325026-0-4

Ebook: 978-1-7325026-3-5

Illustrations by Melissa Damon

Roberta M. Damon

Dear Abishag

Letters to Little Known
Women of the Bible

Oviedo, Florida

HIGHERLIFE
PUBLISHING & MARKETING

DEDICATION

To the women whose names appear in God's Holy Word,
To those who read it,
To those who believe it,
To those who study it,
To those who teach it,
To those who live it.

ACKNOWLEDGMENTS

I extend my gratitude to the great cloud of witnesses, which now includes so many of my dear ones: family members, old friends, missionary colleagues, Brazilian brothers and sisters in Christ, and laborers together in many churches.

And those who remain:

- Del Ray Baptist Church youth group members of the 1950s

- Mars Hill College and Oklahoma Baptist University friends

- Seminary colleagues and professors at Southwestern

- Beloved Brazilians who allowed us to serve among them

- First Baptist Church, Richmond, Virginia, who welcomed me on staff

- The International Mission Board Home Office staff

- Chester Baptist Church and its dear people

Special thanks to:

- Gladys Sherman Lewis, my first editor and publisher and friend of many years

- Patricia Jones, my "techie elf" who knows about computers and gets me where I need to go

- Joyce Clemmons, who has agreed to make all commercial announcements at book signings

- All the great folks who have invited me to speak at their events: you know who you are.

- My family, who has been supportive and encouraging throughout the writing process

- Melissa, who does clever illustrations

- Bill, to whom I have been married for sixty years! God bless you!

TABLE OF CONTENTS

INTRODUCTION

Just about everyone knows Mary, the mother of Jesus. The Christian liturgical calendar includes Advent and Christmas, ensuring that a good portion of the world population will hear her story yearly. Anyone who attended Sunday School as a child will remember stories about Eve, Sarah, and Rachel. Most church folks know about the New Testament sisters, Mary and Martha. But who remembers the story of Abishag or Athaliah? Who can identify Damaris? Who knows the Old Testament character, Jemimah? (No, she is not the one who makes pancakes.)

Many women in Scripture are obscure. They might be mentioned by name, but their stories are not easily recalled, often because there is scant information about them in the Bible. You might remember Phoebe, the woman who delivered Paul's letter to the church in Rome. Did you know that her name means "moon" and that she came out of the pagan worship of Diana, the moon goddess?

This book introduces you to thirty named women of the Bible whom you may or may not recognize. The sections are hardly long enough to be called chapters, but they include Scripture, a letter to a female Bible character, and an acrostic on the name of each woman. Finally, a section under the title "Reflecting" provides questions to stimulate discussion or encourage further study. Whether you use this book as a personal devotional resource for thirty consecutive days or in a study group for thirty sessions, my desire is that you become acquainted with these women and their stories. The New International Version of the Bible is used throughout this book, except where otherwise indicated in the text.

Through this study, you will be reminded that the written Word covers thousands of years and many different cultures. This means that the culture of Genesis differs greatly from the time of Ruth. And all Old Testament stories happened hundreds or thousands of years before Mary and Martha welcomed Jesus into their home in the first century AD. You will do well to place each character's story in its historical context. Did this person live in the time of the judges? Who was king when a particular woman lived her story? Certainly, you will be aware that Old Testament characters will differ greatly from those in the New Testament. Exactly when did Peter pray to raise Tabitha from the dead? When did Orpah live?

In this age of computers, information is available immediately at our fingertips. Your study of this book will be greatly enhanced if you make the effort to learn about the background of the characters. Find out about Moab. Find a history of the building of Solomon's temple. What was so special about purple dye? Why was David's reign so important? What was the role of a prophetess such as Huldah? Why was it so important for women to bear sons? May God's blessings be yours as you read, study, learn, and apply His Word to your life.

Chapter 1

ABISHAG

"When King David was very old, he could not keep warm even when they put covers over him. So his attendants said to him, 'Let us look for a young virgin to serve the king and take care of him. She can lie beside him so that our lord the king may keep warm.' Then they searched throughout Israel for a beautiful young woman and found Abishag, a Shunammite, and brought her to the king. The girl was very beautiful; she took care of the king and waited on him, but the king had no sexual relations with her" (1 Kings 1:1–4).

Dear Abishag,

You must have been beautiful indeed in the days of your youth. As King David's health declined, people knew the old man was dying. His servants piled clothing on him in his bed to give him body heat, but still he was cold. So his servants suggested the idea of scouring the countryside for a beautiful young virgin who would attend to the king's needs and lie beside him to give him body heat. The hope was, of course, to extend his life and keep him comfortable and happy. The CFBV (The Committee to Find a Beautiful Virgin) met and must have divided the country into sections so committee members each had an assignment. I picture them scurrying to find just the right girl. And someone found you! Did they have some sort of beauty pageant to weed out the less desirable virgins? Did they cast Urim and Thummim to select you? We'll never know, but bed duty for King David must have been considered a great honor.

You are from Shunem, are you not? I have to wonder what your dad thought of your new job. As a matter of fact, your name means "my father is a wanderer" or "my father goes astray." It comes from the Hebrew *ab*, which means "my father," and *shagah* means "to go astray or err." Now that's a strange name to give to an infant daughter. Was your father guilty of adultery or some other sin or crime? What did your mother think of your name? Did she agree to name you Abishag to perpetuate your father's shame?

Wherever you went, when people heard your name for the first time, they must have done a double take and asked, "Why did your parents name you that? Just what did your father do?" If they didn't ask out loud, they must have wondered. No matter. You were judged the fairest in the land, and you were taken from your home in your city to King David's bedchamber.

Scripture indicates that you "cherished the king and ministered to him." You must have had a kind heart. Attending to an ailing elderly person is never easy. For a young woman barely out of puberty to be so attentive is remarkable. The goal, as far as the palace staff was concerned, was to arouse the king to perform sexually, a sure sign of vitality. King David was so far removed from that particular activity that he must have caused consternation among those hoping he would recover his vigor and remain in power. David had eight wives and no telling how many concubines. He fathered nineteen sons and no one knows how many daughters (only Tamar is named).

> *What remains is the fact that women are used.*

He was probably absolutely worn out by the time you got around to "cherishing" him. As long as you did what was required of you and David survived, the kingdom remained in a precarious state, to be sure, but it had not yet crumbled into utter chaos.

Sure enough, when the many sons of David heard that their father was dying, the divisions multiplied. Adonijah was on one side against Solomon, Nathan the prophet, and Bathsheba. The three of them verbally assaulted the tired old king until he might have preferred quiet death to their continued yammering. I don't know if David died trying to summon the energy to do what was required or died from exhaustion listening to Bathsheba screeching that David had promised that her son, Solomon, would succeed him on the throne.

Finally, David relented. Adonijah was rejected, and Solomon was anointed as the new king. Not long after, Bathsheba came to Solomon with a request. It had to do with you, Abishag. Bathsheba petitioned the new king to allow Adonijah to take you as his wife. Solomon refused the request, probably because the man, who had the king's harem, might try again to ascend to the throne. Not only did Solomon refuse to give you to Adonijah; he also sent a hit man to kill him. Never mind that they were half-brothers. After that, you disappear from the scriptural account without ever having spoken one word. You, like so many of your sisters, had no voice.

Dear, kind, beautiful Abishag! What happened to you? Where does one go after being honored so young? What does one do when the applause dies? Did you spend the rest of your life telling anyone who would listen, "Oh, yes, I was judged the most beautiful girl in all the land. I was chosen to attend King David." If you had lived in my day, you would have photo albums bulging with snapshots and press releases: "Abishag Wins Beauty Contest." "King Cuddling with Abishag!" "All Bets Are on Abishag."

The kind of fame you experienced is fleeting. The world moves on. We grow older, and other beautiful younger women take their turn in the spotlight. The glory and adulation from a fickle public does not remain. What remains is the fact that women are used, and their physical beauty is exploited for someone else's political and financial gain.

Change comes slowly and painfully. In my day, women are finding a voice. They are speaking out against exploitation, harassment, and domestic violence. Even so, the rape statistics are horrific, and human trafficking is a billion-dollar industry in my country. We make progress, but it is a long time coming. Violence toward women and the continued demeaning of the female body provide a commentary on just how far we have to go to protect and empower our women and girls.

A-fter all, Abishag, because of your

B-eauty you were exploited.

I-n no way

S-hould any girl ever

H-ave to do what you were expected to do.

A-lways remember how valuable you are:

G-od's very own child.

REFLECTING

1. Have you ever been forced or manipulated into doing something you didn't want to do? What emotions did you feel?

2. In your opinion, is there a power differential in our culture between men and women? How has that changed over time?

3. How have Christians helped alleviate human suffering around the world?

Chapter 2

AHINOAM

"Abigail quickly got on a donkey and, attended by her five female servants, went with David's messengers and became his wife. David had also married Ahinoam of Jezreel, and they both were his wives" (1 Sam. 25:42–43).

Dear Ahinoam,

Being David's wife could not have been easy with all the attending intrigue that position entailed. Polygamy has always interested me. I wonder how one wife feels when other wives are added. Don't tell me no one was ever jealous. Remember Sarah and Hagar. In the Old Testament stories, there was often some grand competition among wives to produce sons.

David eventually had eight wives and nineteen sons, and no one knows how many daughters. Of course, David was an amateur compared to his son, Solomon, who had seven hundred wives, many of whom he probably wouldn't have recognized outside the palace.

David's first wife was Michal, daughter of King Saul. Because of Saul's hatred, he took her from David and gave her to another man. You were David's second wife. We know nothing of your courtship or even if there was a courtship. Your marriage might have been a political move of some sort. We do not know how you and David met or exactly when you married. In fact, the King James Version seems to indicate that David married you just after he married Abigail: "And Abigail hasted, and arose...and she went after the messengers of David, and became his wife. David also took Ahinoam of Jezreel; and they were also both of them his wives" (1 Samuel 25:42–43, KJV). The New International Version uses the past perfect tense, which reads, "David had also married Ahinoam of Jezreel," which indicates that you got there first.

If you were ever heartbroken over your husband's behavior, I can only imagine what you suffered because of your son.

Though we know almost nothing of you, Abigail's story is recorded in minute detail. David wasted no time in marrying her. As soon as David heard that her husband had died, he hastened to make her an offer of matrimony. Abigail impressed David while she was still married to Nabal. She was beautiful, generous, competent, and wise. I can guess that she was gracious toward you. I hope you were not threatened by her excellence. Scripture does not indicate that you and she were rivals.

We do know that you presented David with his firstborn son, Amnon. If there was a competition between you and Abigail, the birth of your boy would have put you in the lead for a while. I am assuming, Ahinoam, that you and Abigail maintained a peaceful coexistence.

Four wives later, both you and Abigail must have suffered humiliation when David became besotted with Bathsheba. By that time, he was king and could, I suppose, do anything he wanted to do. What he wanted to do involved intrigue, violence, and bloodshed. As for you, Ahinoam, I wonder if you lived long enough to see your son, Amnon, killed in retribution for raping his half-sister, Tamar. If you were ever heartbroken over your husband's behavior, I can only imagine what you suffered because of your son. The drama of your life is more than anyone should be required to bear. Might you have been happier married to a simple farmer?

A- wife of David you were, no matter

H-ow many other wives followed.

I-ndeed, we must remember that you and

N-o one else produced his first son (the first of many to be sure).

O-ften overlooked,

A-lways in the shadows,

M-ay you rest in eternal peace from all earthly sorrow.

REFLECTING

1. What is your major source of joy?

2. How heavily do you invest in friendships?

3. What experiences have bonded you in friendship, in marriage, in parenting?

4. What have been your greatest disappointments?

5. How difficult is it for you to forgive? Does the memory of old wounds still come back at times?

6. What sort of person were you in times past? How has wounding changed you?

7. What would you tell someone who is in a difficult marriage?

8. How did your family of origin affect the adult you have become?

9. How has the early dynamic of your family informed the relationships you have now?

Chapter 3

ATHALIAH

"When Athaliah the mother of Ahaziah saw that her son was dead, she proceeded to destroy the whole royal family. But Jehosheba, the daughter of King Jehoram and sister of Ahaziah, took Joash son of Ahaziah and stole him away from among the royal princes, who were about to be murdered. She put him and his nurse in a bedroom to hide him from Athaliah; so he was not killed. He remained hidden with his nurse at the temple of the Lord for six years while Athaliah ruled the land" (2 Kings 11:1–3).

Dear Athaliah,

Perhaps I should address you as "Queen Athaliah." After all, you were the only woman to reign as a monarch of Israel or Judah in biblical history. The scriptural account of your family is somewhat confusing. Either King Omri or his son, King Ahab, was your father. You married King Jehoram. None of these is exactly a household name, although most people would remember Ahab as having Jezebel as his wife. You were the mother of Ahaziah. When your husband died, Ahaziah was king for one year. Scripture records that "his mother encouraged him to act wickedly" (2 Chron. 22:3). You probably advised him to forsake Jehovah for Baal worship and fertility practices.

Your son, Ahaziah, was killed in a struggle for the throne. When you learned of his death, you set about killing every person, adult and child, in the royal line of succession. You seized the throne and reigned for the next six years. You had no idea that your grandson, two-year-old Joash, had been saved by Jehosheba, your dead husband's sister. I strongly suspect your sister-in-law didn't like you very much. At first, she hid Joash and his nurse in a bedroom. Then she took the child into the house of the Lord and kept him hidden during the six years of your reign.

When you learned of his death, you set about killing every person, adult and child, in the royal line of succession.

In the seventh year, the priest, Jehoiada, called the captains of the guard and the rulers in the land and showed them the now seven-year-old Joash, the king's surviving son. The leaders made a vow to put Joash on the throne. King David's spears and shields were displayed in the temple. The guards and rulers took them and stood guard along the walls of the temple and by the altar. They brought Joash from hiding, crowned him, swore their allegiance, and anointed him with oil. They clapped their hands and shouted, "God save the king!" You heard all the commotion, Athaliah, and went to the temple and saw that the coronation had already taken place. That's when you ripped your garments and screamed, "Treason!" Priest Jehoiada had made a covenant involving the Lord, the king, and the people. From that day forward, the people would follow the Lord.

The crowd went into the house of Baal and destroyed it. Altars and images were broken into pieces. They killed Baal's priest in front of the altar. They took Joash from the temple to the palace and set him on the throne. Everyone rejoiced. The city was quiet. That's when they executed you. Jehoiada ordered the guard to take you out of the temple to be killed. And that's what happened. Your blood did not defile the house of the living God.

How unutterably tragic that your greed cost the lives of all those in the royal family. How sad that your name is synonymous with selfishness and violence.

A-version is what we feel.

T-o think that you slaughtered your grandchildren!

H-atred, greed, and

A-buse of power

L-ed you to your doom.

I-n history you go down as the

A-ntithesis of all that is good.

H-orrible, selfish, and treacherous woman.

REFLECTING

1. How would you define evil?

2. What do you understand about power grabbing?

3. Why does evil flourish in our world?

4. Do you believe Satan is still the prince of this world? What do you see as his work?

Chapter 4

BILHAH AND ZILPAH

*"Then she (Rachel) said, 'Here is Bilhah, my servant.
Sleep with her so that she can bear children for me and I
too can build a family through her.' So she gave him her
servant Bilhah as a wife" (Gen. 30:3–4, addition mine).*

*"When Leah saw that she had stopped having
children, she took her servant Zilpah and gave
her to Jacob as a wife" (Gen. 30:9).*

Dear Bilhah and Zilpah,

Where did you come from? Did the family of Jacob
purchase you? Were you, like Hagar, from Egypt, or
were you from some other country? You were the maids
for Rachel and Leah. I don't know everything that was
in your job description, but sleeping with the husband
of your mistress sounds a bit beyond the call of duty.
Or maybe it was your duty. We read in Scripture the

account of Hagar's bearing a child for Sarah, so I suppose the concept was not foreign to you.

Few women in the ancient world had much power. Most of them—mothers, wives, daughters, and female servants—were totally dependent on men for survival. As you well know, women were property—owned, managed, confined, illiterate. Home was their world. Of the larger world of politics, religion, finance, philosophy, and influence, they knew nothing. This applied as much to women of high class like Leah and Rachel as to the two of you. When Rachel was found to be barren, it was her decision to tell her husband to impregnate you, Bilhah, so that your child could give her some status. The same was true when Leah, after bearing a number of children, for some reason did not get pregnant again for a time. Then she was the one to tell Jacob to impregnate you, Zilpah. Neither of you had the power to object or resist. And Jacob was certainly a busy boy.

Neither of you had the power to object or resist.

Life is not fair. Life is not equitable. I want to say how sad I feel when I think of how trapped you were in a system that exploited you and so many others. I also want to say that for a majority of people in this world, things have not changed much. There are still people who are privileged and people who live in poverty—the haves and the have-nots. There are those who are exploited and those who grow rich by exploiting others. There are, in my world, people who live in fine homes and those who are homeless. There are children who go to expensive schools and those whose schools are crumbling. There are people of influence and privilege and those who have no voice at all. In my beloved country, we have a phrase we love to repeat: "Liberty and justice for all." I wish it were true. Perhaps, someday, it will be.

B-ecause you were a maid—a slave,

I-nequity was all you knew.

L-ittle valued,

H-aving no power,

A-lways disparaged, you did what you

H-ad to do.

Z-ilpah, you were

I-nsignificant, known only as

L-eah's maid.

P-ower came not to you, but to Leah
    instead.

A sad commentary on the way things
    were as you

H-ad sons for her.

21

REFLECTING

1. Name some inequities in our world.

2. What are some ways your church is involved in helping others?

3. What are you doing on a personal level to make the world a better place?

Chapter 5

CLAUDIA

*"Do your best to get here before winter. Eubulus
greets you, and so do Pudens, Linus, Claudia, and
all the brothers and sisters" (2 Tim. 4:21).*

Dear Claudia,

I have greatly admired you through the years. I well
remember when my friend and missionary colleague,
Carolyn Plampin, told me you appear in Scripture only
one time in Paul's second letter to
Timothy, the very last thing Paul wrote.
She added, "We must find Claudia in
history." So I set out to research your
story. I found you in the writings of the
old Roman poets and historians: Martial,
Suetonias, Tacitus, and Juvenal. Here are some of the
things I found out about you:

> *You began life as
> a British princess
> named Gladys.*

- You began life as a British princess named
  Gladys. Your father, Caradoc, was king of

Siluria, now Wales. When Claudius was emperor of Rome, he put together the greatest of all the Roman expeditionary forces to conquer Britain and make her part of the Roman Empire. Your father held off the Roman legions for seven years. He was never conquered but was betrayed by a kinswoman who favored Rome over Britain. Your family was carried into Rome and was marched through the streets in humiliation.

- When your father (whom the Romans called Caractacus) stood in the Roman Senate to plead his own case, you bravely stood with him, the first woman ever to stand in that place. Emperor Claudius granted your father clemency and then turned to you and said that from now on you were his daughter. He renamed you "Claudia," after himself.

- You married Rufus Pudens Pudentia, a Roman senator and some believe a half-brother to the apostle Paul. You bore four children: Timotheus, Novatus, Praxedes, and Pudentiana. You and your husband were cofounders of the Gentile church in Rome. His villa—your home—was called "Apostolorum," "Paladium Britanicum," "Titulus," and "Pastorum," in turn. It was the center of Christian worship, and all Christians who visited Rome, including both Peter and Paul, stayed there on occasion. You were the only member of your immediate family to die a natural death. Your husband and all four of your children were martyred in the cause of Christ.

When I visited Rome, I went to the church of Saint Pudentiana, named for your younger daughter. It is built over your first-century home. My dear Claudia, you fed and clothed the needy. You visited the incarcerated. You wrote hymns and poems. You were a faithful and loving wife and mother. You lived an exemplary life of Christian virtue. All this you did in turbulent times.

On my trip to Rome, I visited cathedrals and monuments, fountains and museums. I visited the Vatican with all its art. I saw the ceiling of the Sistine Chapel. I saw the Pieta in St. Peter's Basilica. Nothing moved me quite as much as the plaque written in Latin on the threshold of the church named for your daughter. Here is the translation:

In this sacred and most ancient of churches, known as that of Pastor, dedicated by Sanctus Pius Papa, formerly the house of Sanctus Pudens, the Senator, and the home of the holy apostles, repose the remains of three thousand blessed martyrs, which Pudentiana and Praxedes, Virgins of Christ, with their own hands interred.

Christians of the twenty-first century owe a debt of gratitude to you, to your family, and to your *first-century* brothers and sisters—all followers of the Way. I found your story so compelling that I wrote a book about it, entitled *Theirs Is the Kingdom*. It is dedicated to all those martyred in the cause of Christ. Thank you, Claudia, and God bless you, good and faithful servant.

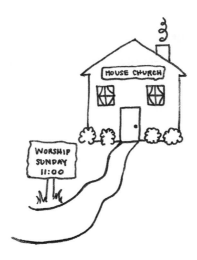

C-ompassionate and kind, you were of royal blood—

L-ovely as a day in

A-pril. You and your dear Pudens,

U-nder Roman penalty of death,

D-edicated your home and children to the Nazarene.

I-n peril, you stood fast:

A monument to Love.

REFLECTING

1. How does your decision to be a Christ follower inform your behavior?

2. Which relationships in your life give evidence of your profession of faith?

3. What does "church" mean to you?

4. How do you feel about the fact that some people around the world are persecuted for their faith?

Chapter 6

DAMARIS

"Some of the people became followers of Paul and believed. Among them was Dionysius, a member of the Areopagus, also a woman named Damaris, and a number of others" (Acts 17:34).

Dear Damaris,

What a privilege to live in Athens, the center of culture for the whole world! You must have loved watching the artists at work in the plazas and shopping in the busy marketplaces. Your city was alive with activity, with its great university and its public debates.

The apostle Paul, on what is known as his second missionary journey, visited your city. While he was waiting for the arrival of his two friends, Silas and Timothy, he walked your streets and listened to debates between philosophers—Epicurians and Stoics. He entered into disputes with Jews in the synagogue, too. People listened to him preach a new belief system. They took him to the Areopagus—the judicial council—

where he made a public speech. In my day, we refer to this as "Paul's Sermon on Mars Hill."

Paul stood and spoke to the gathered crowd: "People of Athens, I see that in every way you are very religious. For as I walked around and looked carefully at your objects of worship, I even found an altar with this inscription: TO AN UNKNOWN GOD. So you are ignorant of the very thing you worship—and this is what I am going to proclaim to you" (Acts 17:22–23).

Then he began by explaining that God created the world. This God is the One in whom "we live and move and have our being" (Acts 17:28a).

To that point in his sermon everyone listened attentively. But when Paul began to speak of Jesus and His resurrection, some of the audience mocked him. Some said they would be willing to hear more about this new religion later. But some believed. You were named as a new believer, along with a man named Dionysius from the town of Areopagus.

While others in Paul's audience rejected the Gospel story, you believed and embraced the Good News with an open heart.

Damaris, I am interested in your appearance at the public speaking. "Respectable" women did not appear in public in Athens in your day. Your identity has been a matter of speculation through the years. Some have suggested that you were the wife of Dionysius. Others think you might have been wife or mother to one the philosophers present. Someone suggested that you must have been a reformed prostitute. In the oldest of manuscripts, the phrase "of high standing" accompanies your name. Might you have been of noble birth?

I'm not sure any speculation about you matters. What we do know about you is that while others in Paul's audience rejected the Gospel story, you believed and embraced the Good News with an open heart.

D-aring to be part of the crowd,

A-ttentive to the

M-essage preached,

A-ware that others scoffed, you

R-ealized the message was for you.

I-n simple trust, you accepted God's great

S-alvation.

REFLECTING

1. Recount your own salvation experience.

2. How have you shared the Gospel story with others?

3. What is the difference between accepting Christ as Savior and growing in grace?

Chapter 7

DINAH

"Then Leah said, 'God has presented me with a precious gift. This time my husband will treat me with honor, because I have borne him with six sons.' So she named him Zebulun. Some time later she gave birth to a daughter and named her Dinah" (Gen. 30:20–21).

"Now Dinah, the daughter Leah had borne to Jacob, went out to visit the women of the land. When Shechem son of Hamor the Hivite, the ruler of that area, saw her, he took her and raped her. His heart was drawn to Dinah daughter of Jacob, and he loved the young woman and spoke tenderly to her" (Gen. 34:1–3).

Dear Dinah,

After your mother, Leah, gave birth to six boys, you were born. She gave you your name. Your family moved to Shalem in the country of Shechem. By the time of that move, you were a beautiful young lady. Scripture records that you went for a walk one day, hoping to meet some other young women, perhaps to make friends with them. That's when Shechem (yes, he had the same name as the country in which you lived), the son of Hamar the Hivite, first saw you.

What happened next has been called a rape; however, considering that the young man treated you with tenderness, there might be another explanation. Rapists are not tender. Rapists are full of rage, and their intent is to harm and control. Some scholars believe that in the ancient world, one of the purposes of a sexual encounter was to create bonding and obligation. Shechem was immediately in love with you. He desperately wanted to marry you to fulfill his obligation to you and to your father. He rushed to ask his own father to negotiate with yours so that a wedding could be arranged.

Your father and your brothers took a dim view of any wedding plans. The males in your family listened to the request. One of the Shechem men said, "Give us your women, and we will give you ours. Let us intermarry, and we will prosper in the land." Your brothers and your father nodded in agreement and said, "There's just one requirement: you must all be circumcised as we are."

"Done," said the men of Shechem.

On the third day after the mass circumcision, while the men were not yet recovered from the pain of the procedure, two of your brothers, Levi and Simeon, came into the city with swords drawn. They killed all the males, including Hamar and his son, Shechem. They plundered the city, taking sheep, oxen, and donkeys. They took captive all the women—wives and daughters, along with the children. They carried off everything that wasn't nailed down.

Your father was not happy. Jacob's reputation was ruined among the population of Canaanites, Hivites, and Perizzites. He reprimanded his sons: "My life is now in jeopardy. You have angered everyone and turned them against me."

Your brothers responded, "What do you expect us to do? Should we let our sister be treated like a harlot?"

God's covenant with Abraham included the stipulation that God would make of Abraham's nomadic people a great nation: "You will be My people and I will be your God" (Ex. 6:1–7). This arrangement precluded marriage with outsiders. I wonder if your brothers reacted, not only to save your reputation, but to obey God's instructions. The way they "protected" you seems excessively violent to a person of my century.

In your culture, marriage was a contract and had nothing to do with being in love.

I am interested that you had no say in the matter of a marriage with the man who fell in love with you at first sight. Of course, in your culture, marriage was a contract and had nothing to do with being in love. And women did not make decisions. Oh, Dinah, your mother named you.

35

Your father and brothers protected you. And you had nothing to say for yourself. You ought to see how women speak up in my culture. You wouldn't believe it!

D-id you return that young man's love for you?

I-f you did, does it matter now? It's

N-ice to have brothers for protection, but still,

A-ll

H-ell broke loose in Shechem.

REFLECTING

1. What do you make of the carnage caused by the brothers of Dinah in this story?

2. How pervasive is violence toward women in American culture in our time?

3. Jesus was called "Prince of Peace." What can Christians do to create a more peaceful world?

Chapter 8

EUODIA
AND SYNTYCHE

"I plead with Euodia and I plead with Syntyche to be of the same mind in the Lord" (Phil. 4:2).

Dear Euodia and Syntyche,

I hope you settled your differences. When Paul wrote that beautiful letter to your church in Philippi, his admonition to you came as a discordant note in an otherwise positive and tender correspondence. His letter was full of grace and gratitude until he decided to instruct the two of you. The letter was written to people Paul called "dearly beloved" (Phil. 4:1, KJV). I'm sure he included you both in that phrase. I think sometimes it might be more difficult to correct those we love than it is to admonish people whom we don't hold dear.

I have no idea what your problem was. Someone suggested that both of your homes may have been "house churches" and that you got into a squabble over that. Was your disagreement over simple turf protecting? I suppose you could have disagreed over doctrine, or maybe it was something personal. No matter. The results could not have been edifying.

Churches are damaged when two strong-minded people publicly disagree. When this happens, it might be that the people in the church try to avoid taking sides. They might be successful for a while but are almost always drawn into the fray. The disagreement might begin over doctrine or ministry but often degenerates into a battle of name calling. No one emerges from such a fight victorious. Churches are always damaged when members engage in discord. Without the unity Paul was pleading for, the church presents a tarnished image to the world. Such behavior gives unbelievers the opportunity to say, "If that's an example of Christian love, I want no part of it."

No one emerges from such a fight victorious.

I like to believe that you forgave one another and went on to work together in harmony as sisters in Christ. Little did you know that Paul's letter to the church at Philippi was to be included in the collection of writings that became our Holy Scripture. I wonder how it felt to find that your disagreement and Paul's reprimand would get "dishonorable mention" and be read by Christians for more than two thousand years? I do hope you managed to get your problem settled.

E-uodia, you engaged in that

U-gly disagreement with your friend.

O-ften we

D-ecide to fight each other

I-n the most unseemly way.

A-mazing grace is better.

S-illy girl!

Y-ou had to have your way.

N-o one knows just what

T-hat spat was all about.

Y-ou upset Paul, and the

C-hurch was upset, too.

H-ow good it is to settle

E-mbarrassing disagreements in peace.

Reflecting

1. Have you ever had a disagreement with a friend?

2. If so, did the disagreement cause a rift in the relationship?

3. Have you ever been angered by another person? How do you handle anger?

4. Is it difficult for you to apologize?

5. What do you believe about forgiveness?

6. How does the animosity between two people spread to include others?

Chapter 9

HEPHZIBAH

"Manasseh was twelve years old when he became king, and he reigned in Jerusalem fifty-five years. His mother's name was Hephzibah. He did evil in the eyes of the Lord" (2 Kings 21:1–2).

Dear Hephzibah,

Your husband was a good king—a very good king. In fact, he was best king Judah ever had! Scripture records that he instituted reforms, tearing down the altars of Baal and requiring all the people of Judah to worship the living God. The history of your era is a series of abrupt changes from one king to the next. A good king ascended the throne, but the next allowed abominations. This happened again when Hezekiah died. Your son, Manasseh, came to power at the tender age of twelve. You never can tell what a pubescent boy will do. Manasseh must have thought frolicking with temple prostitutes might be more fun than keeping God's list of "thou shalt nots."

When a child misbehaves in public, the parents are often blamed. I remember my own parents' oft-repeated warning, "Behave yourself. What you do reflects on us." I must say, I was a good child who struggled mightily not to sully the family reputation. Obviously, Manasseh had no such qualms. You, Hephzibah, must have been heartbroken as you saw the trajectory Manasseh chose. Your pain changed to alarm as your son's decisions catapulted Judah into the depths of heathenism. Did he not remember the story of Elijah and God's victory over the prophets of Baal?

Manasseh reigned for fifty-five years. Not only did he build up the high places his father had destroyed, but he "bowed down to all the starry hosts and served them" (2 Kings 21:3b). He built pagan altars and placed them inside Solomon's temple. He set a graven image inside the temple walls. I wonder if he heard the voice of Jehovah thundering, "Thou shalt not make unto thee any graven image!" (Ex. 20:4, KJV).

He seduced God's people to do more evil than the nations the Lord had destroyed.

Apparently not. During your son's reign, Scripture states, "He has done more evil than the Amorites who preceded him and has led Judah into sin with his idols" (2 Kings 21:11). He seduced God's people to do more evil than the nations the Lord had destroyed.

You might have been an old, old woman when the captains of the host of the king of Assyria carried Manasseh, bound, into Babylon. He was tortured there, helpless and despairing. In his darkest hour, he turned to the Lord, humbled himself, and prayed. God heard his supplication and brought him again to Jerusalem into His kingdom. "In his distress he sought the favor of the Lord his God and humbled himself greatly before the God of his ancestors. And when he prayed to him, the Lord was moved by his entreaty and listened to his plea; so he brought him back to Jerusalem and to his kingdom. Then Manasseh knew that the Lord is God" (2 Chron. 33:12–13).

I'm glad the story has a happy ending. I hope you lived long enough to see the change in your son. I have to wonder about all the damage that had been done and how much healing was needed. Then I remember words written not many years before Manasseh's reign: "If my people, who are called by my name, will humble themselves and pray and seek my face and turn from their wicked ways, then will I hear from heaven, and I will forgive their sin and will heal their land" (2 Chron. 7:14).

H-ephzibah,

E-verything changed. You had no

P-eace when your husband,

H-ezekiah, died at the

Z-enith of his reign.

I-nstead, Manasseh worshipped

B-aal, instituting every

A-bomination. Finally, he

H-umbled himself, and God forgave
him.

REFLECTING

1. Have you, or someone you know, found God out of deep despair?

2. When have you prayed that God would heal our land?

3. What can we learn from the story of Manasseh?

Chapter 10

HERODIAS

"Now Herod had arrested John and bound him and put him in prison because of Herodias, his brother Philip's wife, for John had been saying to him: 'It is not lawful for you to have her'" (Matt. 14:3–4).

Dear Herodias,

You were certainly a piece of work. You could have won first place in a manipulation and scheming contest. You dumped your husband, Philip, so you could marry his brother, King Herod. You always wanted to be queen, and finally you were. You had your way. I wonder how many people were wounded in that process—not that you cared. I imagine Herod was attracted to your fire and passion. Little did he know that passion could become incessant nagging. His attraction might have cooled when you began to pester him about doing something to get even with John the Baptist.

You must have been in a fine rage when John showed

up at your wedding reception uninvited. Instead of toasting the happy couple with champagne, he made a speech in which he upbraided Herod in somber tones. John reminded Herod that it was against Mosaic Law for a man to marry his brother's wife while the brother lived. John ruined your party!

And if you were trying to foist yourself off as the sweet bride, it didn't work. Mark's Gospel says you wanted to kill John, and you would have done it, had your new husband not restrained you. Herod knew John had some kind of power that attracted the support of the masses. I suppose Herod thought, "Better not to have a public uprising." So Herod had John thrown into prison.

Most weddings create a certain amount of stress. Yours was an absolute nightmare.

And then you had the bright idea to celebrate Herod's birthday with a party. I can't believe you involved your own daughter in that event! You managed to get Herod drunk enough to promise anything. And after the exotic dance by your nubile young daughter, Herod, to the surprise of no one, drunkenly exclaimed, "That was some dance, Salome! I will give you whatever your little heart desires to the half of my kingdom. Come over here and sit on your old stepdaddy's lap, and tell me how I can reward you for that pretty little dance."

Of course your daughter went running to you to find out what she should request. After you told her what to say, she ran back to Herod and parroted your words: "I want John's head on a platter." The Lord High Executioner did his job. With one quick stroke of the sword, John's head was severed from his body, placed on a charger, and set, still dripping blood, at Herod's feet. Wasn't that a dainty dish to set before the king?

You give all women a bad name.

So, Herodias, you go down in history as an evil woman who would do anything, including murder, to get her way. I wonder if your DNA might reveal your family relationship to Jezebel? What a legacy! You give all women a bad name.

H-ell hath no fury like a woman reprimanded.

E-ven if John hadn't ruined your party, you

R-eacted to him with rage and wanted him dead.

O-f all your selfish acts, John's

D-eath, and the sight of his head on a charger,

I-s a lasting reminder of the evil you did.

A-s for your legacy, Herodias, eternal

S-hame!

Reflecting

1. Have you known a thoroughly self-centered person?

2. What do you think is meant by a "see, want, get" personality?

3. Manipulation is often a part of an unhealthy relationship. What do you understand about manipulative behavior?

4. Some people "use" others for their own gain. Have you seen examples of how this happens in public life? And in your own experience?

Chapter 11

HULDAH

"Hilkiah the priest, Ahikam, Akbor, Shaphan, and Asaiah went to speak to the prophetess Huldah, who was the wife of Shallum son of Tikvah, the son of Harhas, keeper of the wardrobe. She lived in Jerusalem in the New District" (2 Kings 22:14).

Dear Huldah,

You were related to Jeremiah, the weeping prophet, were you not? You were both descendants of Joshua by his wife, Rahab. While Jeremiah preached repentance to men, you preached the same message to women. You were both prophetess and teacher, well established when Josiah was king of Judah.

Josiah was a good king and a good man. This is surprising because his father, Amon, was not good at all. Amon was a worshiper of Baal, and under his leadership, the worship of the one true God had almost disappeared. Almost everyone in Judah worshipped Baal.

The groves and high places of fertility practices flourished throughout the land. Josiah was only eight when he ascended the throne, but by the time he was sixteen, he had ordered the exclusive worship of YHWH. All pagan forms of worship were forbidden by law. The emblems of Baal were removed from the temple at Jerusalem. Josiah ordered the bones of the dead priests of Baal exhumed and burned on their own altars. He reinstated the celebration of Passover, and the Ark of the Covenant was returned to the temple.

When Josiah was twenty-six, he ordered the temple repaired. Hilkiah the priest found a copy of the book of the law in the rubble. He gave it to Shaphan the scribe, who read it to the king. When *You executed your office with integrity.* Josiah heard the reading of God's Law, he trembled and tore his clothes. He formed a committee and said, "Go and inquire of the Lord for me and for the people and for all Judah about what is written in this book that has been found. Great is the Lord's anger that burns against us because those who have gone before us have not obeyed the words of this book; they have not acted in accordance with all that is written there concerning us" (2 Kings 22:13).

That's when Hilkiah and his committee came to you, Huldah. They asked you, "Will God destroy us?"

Your answer gave them much comfort: "This is what the Lord, the God of Israel, says," you began in authoritative tones. "Tell the man who sent you to me, 'This is what the Lord says: I am going to bring disaster on this place and its people...Because they have forsaken me and burned incense to other gods, my anger will burn against this place...[but to Josiah]: Because your heart was responsive and you humbled himself before the Lord...and wept in my presence, I also have heard you...I will gather you to your ancestors, and you will be buried in peace'" (2 Kings 22:16–20).

You gave a good answer. After King Josiah heard it, he made a covenant to walk after the Lord, to keep His commandments and his testimonies and statutes with all his heart and soul, and to follow all that is written in the book of the law.

You did well, Huldah. You executed your office with integrity. You gave needed words of encouragement to a young king who needed reassurance. You were committed to the one true God. You exemplified the characteristics that are pleasing to the Lord. May we follow in your footsteps with grace and fidelity.

H-eaven gave you the gift of prophecy, of

U-nderstanding. You were

L-oyal to the Lord.

D-elivering His Word to those who sought it,

A-ll found justice. Some found mercy.

H-appy were those who heeded your counsel.

REFLECTING

1. When in your life have you had a spiritual awakening?

2. Can you think of "other gods" we sometimes pursue?

3. What are some characteristics Huldah displayed that we might do well to emulate?

4. How important is the study of Scripture for you? How do you find yourself applying Bible truths to your daily life?

Chapter 12

JAEL

"Jael went out to meet Sisera and said to him, 'Come, my lord, come right in. Don't be afraid.' So he entered her tent, and she covered him with a blanket...But Jael, Heber's wife, picked up a tent peg and a hammer and went quietly to him while he lay fast asleep, exhausted. She drove the peg through his temple into the ground, and he died" (Judg. 4:18, 21).

Dear Jael,

You certainly made a name for yourself in Israel. I suppose your husband, Heber, was off fighting the Canaanites, but as things turned out, you didn't need his help when Sisera, the Canaanite general, showed up at your tent flap. I imagine you had no idea that you would be the subject of song, not only as a conquering warrior, but as fulfillment of prophecy. Your story begins with Deborah, the judge and prophetess.

Deborah called on Barak to raise an army to fight the Canaanites. She promised that she would lure the

Canaanite general, Sisera, to the River Kishon, where she would deliver him into Barak's hands. Barak agreed with the stipulation that Deborah would accompany him to battle. Deborah bluntly warned Barak that he would not be honored when the battle was won because the Lord would deliver Sisera into the hands of a woman. I always thought that meant Deborah would be honored, but that was not the case. It was you, Jael, who was hailed as a heroine.

You were in your tent while the battle raged: Sisera's nine hundred iron chariots against ten thousand Hebrew soldiers. The Lord intervened, and Israel prevailed. Every Canaanite soldier was felled, and Sisera escaped on foot. That's where you entered the story. You were fearless. You met him in the road and sang a siren song: "Come in, come in. Don't be afraid."

You drove the peg through both his temples into the ground.

You covered Sisera with a blanket like a mother covering a sleepy child. He asked for a drink of water. You gave him milk. He instructed you that if anyone came to your tent, asking if there were a man inside, you were to look innocent and answer, "No." Sisera was weary and was soon fast asleep. You quietly picked up a tent peg and a hammer and went softly to him. You drove the peg through both his temples into the ground. The King James Version says, "So he died." (Judg. 4:21, KJV). I guess so!

You stepped outside the tent and met Barak, who was hot on Sisera's trail. You called Barak into your tent, where you showed him what was left of the man he was seeking. I'm thinking that's when Barak thought, "Oh, yes. Now I remember: Deborah prophesied that Sisera would be dispatched at the hands of a woman, and I wouldn't get credit for winning this battle."

Later, Deborah and Barak sang your praises. They embellished a bit, and according to their song, you became an aggressive warrior. They skipped the part about Sisera's being asleep and sang instead, "She put her hand to the nail and her right hand to the workmen's hammer; and with the hammer she smote Sisera, she smote off his head...At her feet he bowed, he fell...he fell down dead" (Judg. 5:26–27, KJV). Your fame spread throughout the land, and you became a mother in Israel. That's some bedtime story to tell your grandchildren!

J-umping Jehosephat!

A-ll you needed was a tent peg and a hammer.

E-veryone thought you were such a nice girl. Then,

L-ights out for Sisera!

55

Reflecting

1. There are those in our day who oppose Christianity. What are some ways we can show strength when we are confronted about our beliefs?

2. What do you fear most?

3. Why are we concerned about getting credit (being praised, getting complimented) for the good we do?

Chapter 13

JEMIMAH

"And he also had seven sons and three daughters. The first daughter he named Jemimah, the second Keziah and the third Keren-Happuch. Nowhere in all the land were there found women as beautiful as Job's daughters, and their father granted them an inheritance along with their brothers" (Job 42:13–15).

Dear Jemimah,

Your name is inscribed in Scripture, along with those of your two sisters, Kezia and Keren-Happuch. Your seven brothers are not named. Can you possibly know how rare and remarkable that is? We find you at the very end of the book named for your father, Job. Your family story is told in the form of a drama. How much of your family history did you know? Did your father ever tell you about what happened to his first family? Oh, yes. He had a family long before you or any of your siblings were born.

Ten children were in that first crop: seven sons and

three daughters, the same number of children you had in your family. Did your father tell you of the terrible day when he lost everything—his flocks, his herds, and worst of all, his ten children? Your father had always been a righteous man. He offered daily sacrifices to God, asking forgiveness for any sins he or his family might have committed. He certainly did not deserve all the terrible losses that came his way. He had not even begun to deal with the shock and grief of his loss when he was struck with a loathsome disease. He very nearly died as he sat on an ash heap, covered from head to foot with pus-filled boils, scraping his body with shards of pottery.

Your father had three long-winded friends who came, ostensibly, to comfort him. They were no comfort.

To think that you and your beautiful sisters inspired an organization helpful to so many gives me joy.

Your father must have winced each time they said, "Come on, Job. You can tell us. What terrible sin have you committed to deserve this calamitous punishment?" Even his wife told him to curse God and die. But your father would not curse God. He remained faithful.

The Bible doesn't tell us, but I think the mother of the ten lost children is not your mother. I think your father married for a second time and that your mother, his new wife, had the second batch of children. I say that because his first wife had borne ten children, and they were grown when the calamity occurred. I think his first wife might have been past her childbearing years by the time your father was recovering. By the time you were born, God had blessed your father with more wealth than he had before.

Scripture indicates that "In all the land were no women found so fair as the daughters of Job" (Job 42:15, KJV). Not only were you beautiful, but your father made provision in his will for you and your sisters, along with your brothers. Your father's provision for you indicates his love and concern for your well-being—a rare gesture for a father toward a daughter in your day.

Jemimah, you will not understand when I tell you that in my day there is a philanthropic organization named for you and your sisters. It is called Job's Daughters. Girls and young women from ages ten to twenty learn character development, reverence for God and Holy Scriptures, and respect for parents. Women who lead the organization teach girls to do good in this world. Job's Daughters will celebrate their centennial in 2020. One hundred years doesn't seem like such a long time when I think of the age of the book of Job, the oldest of the books in our Bible. To think that you and your beautiful sisters inspired an organization helpful to so many gives me joy. I think your father would approve.

J-ust once, Lord, help me understand this world of pain.

E-veryone sometimes aches with loss and grief.

M-ultitudes suffer agony and sorrow.

I want to know why it has to be.

M-aybe, as we walk by faith, the

A-nguish Jesus suffered reminds us that

H-e knows and cares—sufficient grace for me.

REFLECTING

1. The book of Job is a drama in which good wins over evil. Do you believe good always prevails?

2. How does the believer explain human suffering?

3. We have heard the expression "the patience of Job." Do you believe Job was patient? What characteristics did Job model?

4. Why do righteous people suffer?

5. Do you believe Job's story has a happy ending?

Chapter 14

JOANNA

"Jesus traveled about from one town and village to another, proclaiming the good news of the kingdom of God. The Twelve were with him, and also some women who had been cured of evil spirits and diseases: Mary (called Magdalene) from whom seven demons had come out; Joanna the wife of Chuza, the manager of Herod's household; Susanna; and many others. These women were helping to support them out of their own means" (Luke 8:1–3).

Dear Joanna,

You are called by name twice in Scripture: both times by Dr. Luke. Once your name appears as one of the women Jesus healed in Galilee early in His ministry. There, you are identified as "the wife of Chuza," King Herod's finance minister. So we know you lived at Herod's court at Tiberius. I wonder what life at court was like for you.

You were probably aware of Herod's adultery with

his brother's wife, Herodias. She was angry because John the Baptist had publicly disapproved of her behavior, so she harped on the subject to Herod until, finally, he had John thrown into prison. Court life was both privileged and cruel. Were you a witness to Salome's dance at her stepfather's birthday party? Were you present when they brought the head of John the Baptist in on a platter? What a birthday present!

We can assume you were a person of some wealth and certainly of a higher social class than most of the male disciples who followed Jesus. What attracted you to that group of rather ragtag folk: an itinerant preacher, several fishermen, a tax collector, and other ordinary people? Your choice to join them was a drastic change from the life you knew at court. Did you leave your husband? If you did, you must have created a scandal. Did you clean out his bank account? Or did you have money of your own? Were you the one who bought Jesus the seamless robe for which the Roman soldiers gambled at the foot of the cross? Did you buy the ointments and spices that were used to embalm His body?

If Jesus and the Twelve were accompanied by "many women who followed him from Galilee," as Luke stated in his Gospel, I have to wonder how much it cost to feed that crowd day after day for three years. I picture you as elegant, kind, generous, a seeker after righteousness.

The second time you are mentioned in Scripture is at

the empty tomb on Resurrection morning. I think of you
and the other women who, after observing the Sabbath,
went to the tomb that first day of the week. I wish I knew
how many women there were in that group. I try to
imagine the rapid change of emotions on that day, which
began with deep sorrow at the task at hand. Your intention
was to embalm the dead body of the One in Whom you
believed—the One you loved. You had left all to follow
Him. Then terror overtook you as an angel asked, "Why
do you seek the living among the dead? He is not here, but
has risen" (Luke 24:5–6, ESV).

When the women lifted their eyes to the angel,
there must have been a dawning belief
that it might be true. He spoke again:
"Remember what he told you, while he
was still in Galilee, that the Son of Man
must be delivered into the hands of sinful
men and be crucified and on the third day rise" (Luke
24:6b–7). There must have been an audible gasp, and then
rejoicing replaced your sorrow.

You were last at the cross and first at the tomb.

Your example blesses us, Joanna. And the examples of
all your sisters who believed also bless us. You were last at
the cross and first at the tomb. You could not testify in a
court of law because you were female. You were considered too emotional and therefore unreliable. Though the
men did not believe you, no one could take from you the
abiding certainty that what Jesus had told you in Galilee

was true. You saw it with your own eyes. You were a witness to the most important event in all of human history!

Joanna, your name means "the Lord is gracious." I know you found it to be true.

J-esus healed you, a wealthy wife from Herod's court.

O-nly this we know and that you were at the empty tomb

A-nd were a faithful follower and supporter of His cause.

N-o Scriptural account tells more.

N-o dialogue, no parable. It is enough.

A small reminder of His love.

REFLECTING

1. To which institutions and causes do you contribute financially?

2. What does it mean to "leave all and follow Jesus"?

3. What do you understand about the Resurrection? Why is it so important in Christian thought and faith?

Chapter 15

JOCHEBED

"Now a man of the tribe of Levi married a Levite woman, and she became pregnant and gave birth to a son. When she saw that he was a fine child, she hid him for three months" (Ex. 2:1–2).

"Amram married his father's sister Jochebed, who bore him Aaron and Moses" (Ex. 6:20).

Dear Jochebed,

Your story is without a doubt one of the best known in all the Bible. Anyone in my generation, who went to Sunday School as a child, listened, wide-eyed, as teachers told of the baby who was in danger of being killed by the pharaoh of Egypt.

We heard how the baby's mother saved his life by putting him in a little basket boat. We thrilled at how the princess came to bathe in the river, found him, and felt sorry for him. We learned that his sister ran to the princess and asked if she would like to have a nurse for the child. We felt like cheering when she called you, his own mother, to take care of him. The story ends when, after the baby had grown enough, you took him to the pharaoh's daughter, and your child became her son. She named him Moses.

No one noticed that you were not mentioned by name in the story, nor was your daughter, nor the princess. Your name occurs only once, and then only in a genealogy that listed the families of Israel as cited above.

You were a good mother and a smart one. You hatched a plan and saved your child's life. You must have had great courage to put your baby among the bulrushes in the river. You anxiously watched to see what would happen. You put your trust in God, a trust well-placed. God, too, had a plan involving your child.

He was first shaped by you, Jochebed—a mother who trusted the Lord.

What would the story of Israel be without the story of Moses? Someone should write an adventure series containing books with titles like this:

- Moses in a Basket Boat
- Moses and the Egyptian
- Moses's Escape to Midian
- Moses and the Burning Bush
- Moses and His Brother Aaron

- Moses and the Plagues of Egypt
- Moses and the Red Sea Crossing
- Moses and the Wilderness Wanderings
- Moses and the Manna from Heaven
- Moses and the Ten Commandments
- Moses Sees the Promised Land

You must have been proud of your boy. The Old Testament books of Exodus, Leviticus, and Deuteronomy tell of his birth, life, and death. He was the great liberator and lawgiver. He was buried in a secret grave on a mountain in Moab by the Lord God Himself. His epitaph is telling: "And there arose not a prophet since in Israel like unto Moses, whom the Lord knew face to face" (Deut. 34:10, KJV). He was first shaped by you, Jochebed—a mother who trusted the Lord.

J-ustifiably terrified

O-f Pharaoh's plan to kill all male Hebrew

C-hildren, you made a small basket boat,

H-eld your child for one brief moment, then, trembling,

E-ntrusted him to God. You did not know what would

B-ecome of him. God had for him

E-ternal purpose corroborated by many a

D-ivine encounter.

Reflecting

1. What characteristics do you see in Jochebed that are worthy of emulation?

2. How do Christian parents influence their children and future generations?

3. What do you remember about positive influences from your parents and grandparents?

Chapter 16

KETURAH

"Abraham had taken another wife, whose name was Keturah. She bore him Zimran, Jokshan, Medan, Midian, Ishbak and Shuah...All these were descendants of Keturah" (Gen. 25:1–4).

Dear Keturah,

We don't know much about you. In the genealogical record of Adam's line to Noah in 1 Chronicles, you are referred to as "Keturah, Abraham's concubine." In the Genesis account, we read that you were Abraham's wife after the death of Sarah. Your six sons were also mentioned, as well as some grandsons. Josephus, the first-century historian, mentioned you in his Antiquities of the Jews, but he doesn't add to our knowledge of you. A commentator named Richard Elliott Friedman called you "the most ignored significant person in the Torah" but neglected to say why you were significant.

I have some questions. You bore Abraham six sons. Did you have daughters as well? So often in biblical genealogical records, only sons are mentioned. Women are occasionally included, but usually we find a litany of "begats" from father to son—just another reminder that girls and women had no identity, no voice, and no power. My other question is more of an observation. After all the drama in Abraham's earlier marriage (Sarah's inability to bear a child, the involvement with Hagar, Ishmael's birth, and Isaac's eventual arrival), you must have been the delight of your husband's later years. In your marriage, Abraham was surrounded by children and grandchildren: yours and those of his concubines. He must have been happy to settle down with a fertile woman who did not complain or create unnecessary drama.

You gave him joy in place of sorrow.

Before Abraham died at the age of 175 years, he bequeathed all he had to Isaac, the child of promise. To his concubines, Abraham gave gifts before sending them away. The Genesis account does not tell us about you after Abraham was buried beside Sarah at Mamre. I hope your children cared for you, supported you financially, and gathered around you as you became frail. I hope you looked back on the years with Abraham and felt satisfaction in the fact that you were the wife he needed. You gave him joy in place of sorrow.

K-eturah, you married an old man, but

E-ven though Abraham was

T-ired and grief-stricken,

U-pon your arrival in his life, the

R-ain stopped

A-nd the sun began to shine. He was

H-usband again—and father!

Reflecting

1. In American culture, expectations of women have changed over the years. What are your observations of this phenomenon?

2. In biblical times, few women had careers outside the home. Some Christians believe this should be a model for families today. What do you think?

3. How do we differentiate between custom (what we consider acceptable behavior) and eternal truths (what God desires of His children)?

Chapter 17

LOIS

"I am reminded of your sincere faith, which first lived in your grandmother Lois and in your mother Eunice and, I am persuaded, now lives in you also" (2 Tim. 1:5).

"And how from infancy you have known the Holy Scriptures, which are able to make you wise for salvation through faith in Christ Jesus" (2 Tim. 3:15).

"He came to Derbe and then to Lystra, where a disciple named Timothy lived, whose mother was Jewish and a believer but whose father was a Greek" (Acts 16:1).

Dear Lois,

There is nothing on this Earth as sweet as being a grandmother. From the moment you discover your child will have a child, little else absorbs your thoughts. Will the child be a boy or a girl? Will the baby have my eyes and Grandpa's smile? Will the baby be healthy? What will the future hold? We love our children, but grand-children are the joy of our later years. Timothy must have been a dear little boy, the delight of your life.

What we know of your family is rather complicated. We know that your daughter, Eunice, was Timothy's mother. Though she was a Jewish convert to Christianity, Timothy's father was Greek. We know that Timothy was not circumcised as a baby because Paul circumcised him when the two of them were dealing with Jews who insisted men were not of God's covenant without that rite. And we know that while Timothy was a young child, you and Eunice taught him the Scriptures. Paul commends both you and your daughter as being women of faith.

The two of you together did a fine job of rearing Timothy in the nurture and admonition of the Lord.

Years ago, when I taught small children in Sunday School, at story time, we showed the children large pictures—an artist's rendition illustrating the Bible story. The artist depicted Timothy to be about five years old, seated on your lap. His mother stood close by. In your hands you held a Torah scroll. You were teaching Bible stories to Timothy. Only much later did I realize that Torah scrolls were rare and unlikely to be owned or handled by private citizens. Generally, the scrolls were handled by rabbis in the temple or synagogue.

Also, I wondered if you and your daughter knew how to read. Many women in the first-century cultures were not educated. Jewish boys received an education and were officially ushered into life as men under the law at the age of thirteen. Girls learned to be good wives and mothers.

When I read what Paul wrote to Timothy, I understood that you and your daughter knew the Scriptures well and shared those Old Testament stories with your grandson. Still, I doubt you had Torah scrolls in your private possession. And the artist, who illustrated those Bible stories I was teaching to my Sunday School children, might have been more accurate deleting the scrolls from the picture. I would have drawn you and Eunice sitting on the floor with Timothy, telling him Bible stories.

You have every reason to be proud of your daughter. She must have learned her lessons well. She was a superb mother to her child and was both loving and attentive to you, her own mother. The two of you together did a fine job of rearing Timothy in the nurture and admonition of the Lord. What joy to take an active part in Timothy's growing-up years! What joy to watch a loved grandchild grow into adulthood, a faithful follower of Jesus!

L-oving grandmother
O-f the child, Timothy, you
I-nstilled faith in him which
S-till blesses us.

Reflecting

1. How did your grandmother influence you when you were a child and through the years?

2. What kind of grandparent are you, or do you hope to be?

3. How important are the earliest influences in a person's life?

4. Name people who had a positive influence on your early life.

5. Who has been a role model or mentor for you in spiritual matters?

6. Who led you to faith in Christ?

Chapter 18

LYDIA

"On the Sabbath we went outside the city gate to the river, where we expected to find a place of prayer. We sat down and began to speak to the women who had gathered there. One of those listening was a woman from the city of Thyatira named Lydia, a dealer in purple cloth. She was a worshiper of God. The Lord opened her heart to respond to Paul's message. When she and the members of her household were baptized, she invited us to her home. 'If you consider me a believer in the Lord,' she said, 'come and stay at my house.' And she persuaded us" (Acts 16:13–15).

Dear Lydia,

You attended the Greater Philippi Evangelistic Crusade led by Paul, Silas, and Timothy. That makes me think of the big-city evangelistic campaigns of my youth led by Billy Graham, Cliff Barrows, and George Beverly Shea. There is something absolutely compelling about hearing the Word plainly and clearly preached. I remember how crowds of people gathered at the

Billy Graham crusades; at his invitation, many stepped forward to profess Jesus as Savior. When you heard the Apostle Paul preach, you accepted the Lord, and you and your household were baptized. What a glorious experience!

You have been the subject of much disagreement. Some say you were a Jewess and that Paul found you attending a Jewish Sabbath worship service beside a stream. A feminist theologian points out that the polytheism of the day might indicate you were involved in goddess worship. Some commentaries state that you were a righteous Gentile or "God-fearer" attracted to Judaism, but not yet a convert. Whatever you were before you heard Paul preach, you were a Christian afterward. You, my dear Lydia, are considered the first convert to Christianity in what is now Europe. All commentaries agree about that.

You, my dear Lydia, are considered the first convert to Christianity in what is now Europe.

You were also quite the independent woman, a well-to-do agent of a firm dealing in purple dye in the city of Thyatira. That dye was used for clothes worn by royalty and the ultra-rich. I imagine you lived well. Scripture indicates that you owned your house. You are numbered with other women who were home-owners—Martha, the sister of Mary and Lazarus, comes to mind. Your household was baptized with you. Because no husband is mentioned in your story, I wonder if you were a widow. There is so much we don't know about you.

My assessment of your personality is intriguing. I see you as bold. After your baptism, you stepped up to Paul and insistently invited the whole evangelistic team to stay at your house for as long as they were in Philippi. The King James Version says you "constrained" them. You were no shrinking violet. I also note your generosity. You were aware that someone had to prepare beds and food for three tired, hungry men. You were cordial in your offer of hospitality.

You were a person of spiritual sensitivity. You attended worship, seeking truth. You must have been enthralled as Paul preached. Luke wrote that the Lord opened your heart, and you became a believer in the Lord Christ. I wonder how many women you influenced over the years of your life. Through God's written Word, your influence remains.

L-ove compelled

Y-ou,

D-ear lady, to extend the

I-nvitation to your home. God gave you

A gift of hospitality.

REFLECTING

1. Have you ever experienced an old-fashioned revival meeting?

2. How do you believe God is at work in our world today?

3. What gifts of the Holy Spirit do you possess?

4. One of Lydia's spiritual gifts was hospitality. Who in your church practices that gift?

Chapter 19

MARY

"Near the cross of Jesus stood his mother, his mother's sister, Mary the wife of Clopas, and Mary Magdalene" (John 19:25).

Dear Mary,

The only time you are mentioned by name in Scripture is in John's Gospel. You are listed in the crucifixion narrative above as one of the women at the cross. The verse is ambiguous, even in the original Greek. Were there three women or four? The answer depends on how the text is read. If we read "Mary the wife of Clopas" as an appositional phrase to the previous phrase, "his mother's sister," there were three. If we read the verse as a simple list, there are four. Mary, whether you were the biological sister of

I wonder if you went home with Mary to help her through that dreadful night.

Mary, the mother of Jesus, or her spiritual sister, you were standing with her in love and support.

As you watched the horror of the crucifixion, you must had been overcome with helpless grief. After Jesus died, His body taken down from the cross and laid in Joseph's tomb, I wonder if you went home with Mary to help her through that dreadful night. I picture the two of you in happier days. I'm sure you laughed together at family stories and remembered family events through the years: Passover meals and feast days. If you had children, they must have grown up with Jesus and His siblings.

I wish I could talk to you and ask you questions. If you were a part of the family, or even if you were a close friend, you would know so much family history. How old was Jesus when Joseph died? What type of relationship did Jesus have with his four brothers? How many girls were in that family? How close was the relationship between Jesus and his cousin, John the Baptist, in their growing-up years? Had Mary confided to you the story of Jesus's birth? When did you first believe that Jesus is the very Son of God? I thank God for the written account we have in our Bible. Did you ever imagine that two of Jesus's disciples, Matthew and John, and others would later write the story? Could you possibly have dreamed that I would be reading about you and everyone else two thousand years after you stood at the cross on that awful day?

All we know with certainty about you is that you were married to Clopas, and you were at the cross on the day Jesus died. I have a theory, though, about what might also be true. I think you were the "companion" who walked with Clopas from Jerusalem to Emmaus. In his account, Luke does not indicate the gender of the companion. Everyone has almost always assumed it was a man. I have two reasons for believing it was you. First of all, you were his wife. I would think Clopas would not leave his wife in Jerusalem and walk home alone. Also, before you knew the "Stranger" who walked with you was Jesus, you invited Him for a meal. I doubt Clopas cooked dinner. You probably prepared dinner.

So many questions remain, Mary. I would like to know with certainty that you walked the road to Emmaus with your husband. I like to think that you listened as the "Stranger" taught you from the Scriptures. I can imagine you in your kitchen preparing a meal that night. I can almost see your reaction as you saw Him break the bread. You and Clopas immediately knew that you had spent much of the day with Jesus, listening as He taught the Scriptures. When He broke the bread and disappeared, you and Clopas must have looked at each other in astonishment. If you were your husband's companion on the road to Emmaus that day, you were among the very first to see the risen Lord.

M-aybe it was you who
A-ccompanied Clopas on the
R-oad to Emmaus. If so,
Y-ou saw the risen Lord.

REFLECTING

1. If you had stood at the foot of the cross with the women, what would have been your thoughts?

2. Do you have friends or family who support you through times of crisis? Name them.

3. How have you shown love and support for others?

Chapter 20

MICHAL

"Now Saul's daughter Michal was in love with David, and when they told Saul about it, he was pleased" (1 Sam. 18:20).

"Saul sent men to David's house to watch it and to kill him in the morning. But Michal, David's wife, warned him. 'If you don't run for your life tonight, tomorrow you'll be killed.' So Michal let David down through a window, and he fled and escaped" (1 Sam. 19:11–12).

Dear Michal,

You didn't take long to fall in love with David, and no wonder. Scripture tells us he was a fine-looking redheaded boy with beautiful eyes. I imagine he was in great shape, too. He had to be to be able to wrestle and kill a bear and a lion when he was watching over his father's sheep. I don't suppose you ever thought you could have him all to yourself. And you were right. David eventually had eight wives, no telling how many concubines, and a multitude of children: twenty we know about, including nineteen sons and Tamar, the only daughter named. We can assume he had other daughters who were neither named nor numbered.

When the Spirit of the Lord had departed from Saul, your father, he was troubled and obsessed with David's popularity. Both you and your brother, Jonathan, loved David and saved his life when your father tried to kill him. Once, when your father threw a javelin at David, he missed as David dodged the spear. The javelin lodged in the wall, and David escaped. Enraged, your father sent messengers to your house with orders to kill David in the morning. You heard about the plot. When David came home, you told him he had to escape that night or be killed.

You let him down through a window and helped him get away. Then you put a household god in the bed, put a pillow of goat's hair at its head, and covered it with a bedspread. When your father's messengers came to kill David, you said, "Sorry. He's sick." They left, but when they returned, they discovered the idol and your ruse. Your father was displeased at your deception, but David was safe, and that was all that mattered to you. You risked your life to save him. You must have loved him very much.

What happened to you, Michal, to change your feelings for David? Remember when David rescued the ark of the Lord and took it home? He sacrificed a bull and a fatted calf, and then, wearing only a linen ephod (which must have looked something like a hospital gown), he danced before the ark "with all his might" (2 Sam. 6:14). You watched from a window, and when you saw him leaping and dancing, you despised him in your heart.

When David and his entourage entered the city, you watched as he gave bread, meat, and wine to everyone in the crowd. When the people dispersed, you went out to meet David, and you spoke to him sarcastically: "Well, the king of Israel certainly distinguished himself today: disrobing in front of all the slave girls like some lowlife." David answered you harshly about his dancing. He said, "It was before the Lord who chose me rather than your father or anyone from his house when he appointed me ruler over the Lord's people Israel—I will celebrate before the Lord. I will become even more undignified than this, and I will be humiliated in my own eyes. But by these slave girls you spoke of, I will be held in honor" (2 Sam. 6:21–22). I imagine you had no adequate response to such a reprimand. And then the next verse says, "Michal daughter of Saul had no children to the day of her death" (2 Sam. 6:23).

This was the ultimate sorrow for any woman in your day, especially for the first wife of a king. When I think of how you saved David from death at your father's hand and how much, as a young woman, you loved him—the shepherd boy who would be king—I'm sad to think of all you suffered in your marriage. Your father first gave you to David and then took you away and gave you to another man. You were restored to David eventually. You saw your husband marry seven more wives. You witnessed a multitude of babies born to them while never having the joy of giving David a son.

I'm sad to think of all you suffered in your marriage.

I don't know what happened to your love for him. Were you worn down by all the wives and concubines, the many sons the others bore? Did the memory of your father's glory turned to dust erode your love? Did the memory of your second husband's broken heart wound you, too? When the beautiful Bathsheba entered the picture, did you agonize over David's antics as he mooned over this woman he wanted so much that he arranged her husband's death?

David's reign as king is still hailed as the golden age of Israel. Oh, Michal, what happened to you?

M-y soul! What life was this?

I cannot bear to think of the young joy, the old pain.

C-rushed by husband, sovereign, betrayer:

H-er only hope to bear sons—dashed,

A-ll was lost.

L-ove died. Her heart turned cold.

REFLECTING

1. What happens in marriages when harsh words are spoken?

2. In our culture, what are the expectations we have of husbands?

3. What is expected of a good wife?

4. What has been your own experience in marriage?

5. What effect do you believe polygamy had on Old Testament families?

Chapter 21

ORPAH

"Now Elimelek, Naomi's husband, died, and she was left with her two sons. They married Moabite women, one named Orpah and the other Ruth. After they had lived there about ten years, both Mahlon and Kilion also died, and Naomi was left without her two sons and her husband" (Ruth 1:3–5).

"At this they wept again. Then Orpah kissed her mother-in-law goodbye, but Ruth clung to her" (Ruth 1:14).

Dear Orpah,

If anyone remembers you, it may be because of Oprah Winfrey. The story may be anecdotal, but I heard that her parents meant to name her after you but inadvertently misspelled the name, so she became Oprah instead of Orpah. She is instantly recognized in my country and probably around much of the world. If only your name were Oprah, you might be equally famous. But alas! Almost no one remembers you.

You were the widow of Kilion, the son of Naomi and Elimelek. Kilion came to Moab with his parents and brother, Mahlon, when there was a famine in their land of Judah. Scripture does not indicate the ages of the two boys at the time of the family's arrival in Moab. Sadly, Elimelek died. Naomi was then the single mother of two boys. When they were of marriageable age, they married "Moabite women": you and Ruth. After ten years, both your husband and your brother-in-law died. You must have grieved for your husband, as Ruth grieved for hers and Naomi grieved. Not only was Naomi a widow; she had also lost her only sons. I can imagine that the three of you became inseparable during that dark, painful time. You must have leaned heavily on each other for comfort and support.

By the time of your loss, you and Ruth had been a part of Naomi's family for ten years. As your story unfolds, we learn that you loved Naomi so much that when she planned to go back to her town of Bethlehem, you and Ruth decided to leave your families in Moab and go with her. Naomi encouraged you both to stay with your people in Moab and to find husbands in your hometown. Weeping, you kissed Naomi good-bye and turned back to your people and your gods.

Knowing a bit about Moab, I must tell you that your decision to stay there gives me cause for concern. The country of Moab bears the name of its founder. The child Moab was born of the elder daughter of Lot after escaping the fire and brimstone of Sodom and Gomorrah. To "preserve the seed" of their father, the two daughters of Lot got him drunk on two successive nights. Both girls became pregnant from this incestuous relationship—an inauspicious beginning for the country of Moab. The chief god of your country was Chemosh, one of the fertility gods. His name means "destroyer" or "subduer." I can't imagine tossing my babies into a fire because my god demanded it. Perhaps while you were married to Kilion, you learned about the God of the Hebrews—the one true God.

> *Perhaps while you were married to Kilion, you learned about the God of the Hebrews—the one true God.*

How I wish you had gone to Bethlehem, too. You would have found a good life there. You might know that Ruth married a man named Boaz. She had a child named Obed. He grew up to be the father of Jesse, who was the father of David, who grew up to be king of Israel. And many, many years after David's reign, there was another child born in Bethlehem of David's house and lineage. They named him Jesus. His coming was the most important event in all of human history. I worry about what might have happened to you in Moab. I wish you had gone to Bethlehem with Ruth and Naomi instead, but I hope you believed in their God.

O-h, Orpah, I think

R-uth chose the better path.

P-erhaps you were safe in Moab

A-nd you found a good life there. I

H-ope you did.

REFLECTING

1. What do you think might have happened to Orpah after the narrative has her turning back to Moab? Do you think she might have been in danger in Moab? Why or why not?

2. What circumstances in your own life have led you to make the decisions you have made?

3. What might you do differently if you could go back in time?

Chapter 22

PENINNAH

"There was a certain man from Ramathaim...whose name was Elkanah...He had two wives; one was called Hannah and the other Peninnah. Peninnah had children, but Hannah had none" (1 Sam. 1:1–2).

Dear Peninnah,

Living as you did with a husband who loved someone else must have been intolerably painful. The "someone else" in your case was Elkanah's other wife, Hannah. He should have loved you more than he loved her. After all, you were the one who produced sons and heirs for him when Hannah could not. Scripture plainly states that Elkanah favored Hannah over you. He gave you and your children "portions," but to Hannah he gave a "double portion because he loved her" (1 Sam. 1:5).

The implication was that he didn't really love you.

The implication was that he didn't really love you.

I will never understand polygamy or why the Lord sanctioned it. Throughout the Hebrew Scriptures, allowing men to have a multiplicity of women seems to have caused nothing but trouble. Polygamy gives new meaning to the term "blended family."

Being unloved does nasty things to people. Unless they are utterly crushed, they become angry, jealous, hateful, vindictive, and self-serving. Unloved and left out, they target those who are cherished and favored. Peninnah, you used the only tool available to you against your adversary: mockery. I can almost hear you now, your voice dripping with sarcasm: "Look, Hannah, at my many children. See how beautiful they are and how intelligent. Watch your husband's eyes light up as his strong sons surround him. See what pleasure he takes in his dear daughters. Too bad you have no children to bring such pleasure to their father. I suppose the Lord has reasons for giving me so many children and giving you none. What a pity! How you must weep because you are barren."

You made Hannah cry with your hateful words. Children in my day have a little singsong response to harsh words aimed to wound: "Sticks and stones may break my bones, but words will never hurt me." That is so untrue! "Sticks and stones may break my bones, but words will break my heart." Hannah couldn't eat. I doubt she slept well. She cried all the time. You had your revenge.

Poor Elkanah! He was caught between his two wives. He had to listen to your complaints about your unhappiness over his love for Hannah. I'm sure you frequently pointed out to him how blessed he should feel to be the father of so many children. You must have mentioned that it was obvious the Lord had favored you and not Hannah. Maybe it would have helped if Elkanah had just said to you, "Honey, there is no reason to be unhappy. Of course I love you, too." But he didn't. And he seemed to spend an inordinate amount of time trying to cheer Hannah: "Don't I mean more to you than ten sons?" (1 Sam. 1:8). Doesn't that sound just like a man!

Peninnah, I wonder what happened to you and your children. It seems to me that when Hannah was finally able to conceive and give birth to her son, Samuel, that the family dynamic might have deteriorated even further. I'm sure the comments in the marketplace went something like this: "Oh, look. Here comes Hannah with her baby boy. Isn't he just the sweetest thing? If you ever doubted the power of prayer, just look at him. Hannah had to wait such a long time for him. Word has it that she dedicated him to God. Hannah certainly deserves this baby. She is just wonderful! Everyone is so happy for her."

I'm not sure "everyone" was all that happy. I wonder if your children resented the intrusion of the new "baby of the family," thereby carrying the resentment toward Hannah and her child to the next generation. I am certain that Elkanah showed favoritism to this new child, granted by the Lord Himself to a previously barren woman.

Who would not glory in the miracle? You. You, Peninnah, would not rejoice. You might find Hannah's newfound fecundity further reason for envy. Your children might have begun to feel as unloved and left out as you had always felt. They must have felt their father's partiality to Samuel. They must have struggled as they sought his approval. Unresolved issues of acceptance or rejection creep into family dynamics from generation to generation—just like the sins of the fathers.

P-oor girl.

E-veryone else was loved.

N-ot her, though.

I-n spite of her producing a goodly brood,

N-o one told her how wonderful she was;

N-o one told her that love is not rationed.

A-t any rate, she seethed with jealousy over

H-annah the beloved—the barren.

REFLECTING

1. What do you know about sibling rivalry?

2. What happens in families in which love is regarded as a scarce commodity?

3. What happens to a child when parental approval is withheld?

4. How do you think love withheld in one generation affects future generations?

5. How does an unloved person tend to parent his or her own children?

Chapter 23

PHOEBE

"I commend to you our sister Phoebe, a deacon of the church in Cenchreae. I ask you to receive her in the Lord in a way worthy of his people and to give her any help she may need from you, for she has been the benefactor of many people, including me" (Rom. 16:1–2).

Dear Phoebe,

Many years ago, when I was a child, my daddy was ordained a deacon in Trinity Baptist Church in Oklahoma City. I remember watching from the pew while the other deacons—all men, of course—laid their hands on my father's head and blessed him. I remember being proud in the years that followed when my dad helped serve the Lord's Supper. He did it better than the other deacons, taking care to fold the white tablecloth just so. I was proud of him. Mere mortals looked upon deacons as special—some superior Christian life form.

In our church, they enjoyed status and prestige.

They were the ones who ran the church. They made all the important decisions about money and personnel. No women served in that body as deacons, but it was my observation that women did the real work of the church. Though not recognized as particularly important, the women taught the children, arranged the flowers, carried casseroles to the sick and bereaved, and cared about poor people. Deacons did the "important" things and were visible in the congregation. Women did the footwork and, for the most part, kept quiet about it.

Phoebe, your name means "moon." You converted to Christianity from paganism. "Phoebe" was one of the names of the moon goddess known to the Romans as Diana. The real meaning of your name is "the bright one" or "the radiant one." Some scholars think you were a woman of independence. You traveled to Rome.

You were a bright woman who radiated the love of Jesus.

Did you have business there? You must have been a person of great competence. Paul entrusted to you the only copy of his letter to the church in Rome—what we know as the book of Romans in our New Testament. Paul must have deemed you trustworthy for so precious a document to be given to you for delivery. Just think! That was the only copy in existence because Paul had no access to a copy machine.

Phoebe, the Apostle Paul commended you to the

church at Rome. He called you "our sister." Then he used a word that has been mistranslated as "servant" in many versions. The word in Greek is diakonos. Paul used it twenty-two times, eighteen of which appear in the KJV as "minister" and three times as "deacon." It is translated "servant" only once, when it applies to you, Phoebe. The 1611 translators could not bring themselves to use the word "deacon" to describe a woman. They translated it as "servant," although in other places, they transliterated the word to read "deacon" when it applied to men.

All of this truly misses the point. The work of a deacon is the same as the work of a servant: serving the communal meal, taking Communion to those unable to attend services, instructing converts, assisting in baptisms, distributing food and funds to the needy, visiting the sick and imprisoned, consoling the bereaved, and caring for orphans. You, Phoebe, were a deacon—a servant—of the church in Cenchreae. Paul asked the church in Rome to give you a Christian welcome. He asked that they help you because you had helped so many—including him.

We have no way of knowing if you were ever ordained a deacon. What difference does it make? You were a bright woman who radiated the love of Jesus. You gave of yourself and honored your Lord with your life and service.

P-leasing to God was your life of service.

H-elping others was what you did,

O-nly hoping to be faithful to Christ.

E–ven when weary, you

B-rought joy and delight. Rest in

E-ternal light, oh radiant one.

Reflecting

1. How do you radiate the light of Christ in your life?

2. How important to you are titles, honor, and public recognition?

3. What do you understand about the offices of deacon, elder, and pastor?

4. What should be the lifestyle of all Christians?

Chapter 24

RAHAB

"Then Joshua son of Nun secretly sent two spies from Shittim. 'Go, look over the land,' he said, 'especially Jericho.' So they went and entered the house of a prostitute named Rahab and stayed there" (Josh. 2:6).

"But Joshua spared Rahab the prostitute, with her family and all who belonged to her, because she hid the men Joshua had sent as spies to Jericho—and she lives among the Israelites to this day" (Josh. 6:25).

Dear Rahab,

The writer of Hebrews included you in the great collection of heroes of the faith. Among believers in the living God, there is no higher accolade. You made the list because you protected a couple of Hebrew spies Joshua sent to gather intelligence in Jericho.

I suppose the spies thought a brothel was an appropriate place to get information. When the king of

Jericho ordered you to hand over the spies, you said, "Two strangers came to my house." Then, pointing, you continued, "They went that way, and if you hurry, you might be able to catch them" (paraphrasing Joshua 2:4). Of course, the men hadn't left. You hid them on your roof under drying stalks of flax.

Before the spies slept, you went up to chat with them. What you said was most remarkable: "Everyone in Jericho is terrified of you. We have heard how the Lord dried up the Red Sea for you, how He defeated kings for you. As soon as we heard this, we began shaking in our boots. Then you gave a ringing declaration of faith: 'The Lord your God, he is God in heaven above and earth beneath.'"

And then you made a deal. "Swear to me by the Lord, since I have been kind to you that you will be kind to me and my family. Swear that when you have taken Jericho, you will save my kindred." *And then you made a deal.* (See Joshua 2:8–13.) The men promised. They instructed you to hang a red cord from your window so that all the Israeli soldiers would be able to identify your house and spare your family. Then you helped them out a window, and they climbed down the city wall. Later, when the battle of Jericho was over and the Israelites were the victors, Joshua cursed the people inside the city gates—everyone except you, Rahab. He sent the two spies back to your house. They evacuated everyone in your family. Afterward, the city was torched.

I am interested in the red cord you hung from your window. Some say it was a symbol of the red-light district. Some say it is reminiscent of the blood of the lamb on the doorposts of the homes of Hebrew slaves in Egypt when the death angel passed over. The cord was red. The blood of the lamb was red. But the greater similarity is that both had saving power. The blood of the lamb saved the Hebrews' firstborn sons. The red cord saved you and your family from death. You were spared from Israel's obligation to destroy all the Canaanites.

You and your family went to live in Israel. You were a foreigner, but you were brought into the Promised Land. You were a woman, but you were included. You were of low estate, but you were honored. Your name appears in Matthew's genealogy of the family of Jesus. Among the many men, only five women are included: you, Rahab the prostitute; Tamar, the rape victim; Ruth, the foreigner; Bathsheba, the adulteress; and Mary, mother of Jesus.

The writer of Hebrews included you, Rahab, in the list of heroes of the faith along with Abraham, Sarah, Isaac, Joseph, and Moses. The Amplified Version states: "By faith Rahab the prostitute was not destroyed along with those who were disobedient, because she had welcomed the spies [sent by the sons of Israel] in peace"

(Heb. 11:31, AMP). To be included and honored is affirming. You were a woman of worth, a part of God's family.

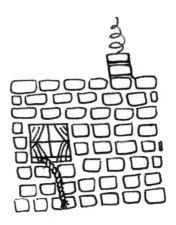

R-ahab, you made an

A-mazing statement of faith in Israel's God:

H-ardly a common thing for a Canaanite to do.

A-ll the same, it saved your life and your family.

B-lessed are you, hero of the faith.

REFLECTING

1. What amazing thing has God done in your family?

2. How has God moved in your life to accomplish His purposes?

3. How can we honor God?

4. If you were adding to the list of heroes of the faith, which modern names would you include?

Chapter 25

RHODA

"Peter knocked at the outer entrance, and a servant named Rhoda came to answer the door. When she recognized Peter's voice, she was so overjoyed she ran back without opening it and exclaimed, 'Peter is at the door!'" (Acts 12:13–14).

Dear Rhoda,

Did you ever hear the story of the pastor who called an emergency prayer meeting during a terrible drought? The congregation gathered to pray for rain. Only one little girl thought to bring an umbrella. You remind me of her.

You lived in perilous times. Jerusalem and all of Israel were under Roman domination. Claudius was emperor of Rome. It must have been around 40 AD. Being a follower of the Way was a capital offense at that time. Christians were being arrested daily and put to death as traitors to the state. Herod Agrippa was king over most of Israel: Judea, the Galilee, and Perea. He curried favor with the Jews by killing James, one of the early disciples of Jesus. You remember him. He was a fisherman, the brother of John, the son of Zebedee. And then Herod had Peter arrested and thrown into prison to the roaring approval of the crowd. Herod curried favor with the Jews by meticulously keeping the law. He enjoyed wide and enthusiastic support.

I know you were present at the prayer meeting at the home of Mary, John Mark's mom. The church gathered to pray for Peter's release and safety. The members of the church might have been so deep in prayer that they didn't hear the knock on the door. But you heard it. Was it your job as a servant girl to answer the door? I can only imagine with what delighted astonishment you heard Peter's voice and ran to interrupt the prayer meeting.

You were accused of being crazy. (What a commentary on lack of faith!) You insisted. They said you'd seen

You rose up and declared what you knew to be true.

Peter's ghost. All this time Peter stood outside knocking. When the church members finally went to the door, they saw Peter, and in their happiness at seeing him, they swamped him with hugs and questions. Then he told them how the angel of the Lord had miraculously taken him out of the prison, how the shackles had fallen from his arms, and how the city gate had opened by itself. And you were there to hear the story of this miracle.

Rhoda, your name is from the Greek. It means

"rose"—a beautiful flower with sweet perfume. In my language, "rose" is also the past tense of the verb "to rise." I want to tell you how much I admire you. You rose up and declared what you knew to be true. You did not waver. That's not easy when everyone else is trying to shout you down. You were right. And you were strong. Finally, everyone present rejoiced at Peter's miraculous escape. Did you ever have the desire to say, "I told you so?"

Scripture does not tell us what happened to you. Did you go singing to your death among other believers? Did you suffer martyrdom in the cause of Christ? I hope you lived a long life and had children and grandchildren whom you entertained with the story of how Peter was prayed out of prison and how you were the only one who had faith that God would answer prayer.

R-are was your faith in God to answer prayer.

H-aving only to believe your

O-wn eyes, you

D-id not waver. Peter really was

A-t the door. You could rightly say, "I told you so."

REFLECTING

1. How do you express your faith?

2. Christians believe in prayer. Are all prayers answered?

3. Do you believe in miracles? Why? Why not?

4. What do you know about the persecution of Christians in our world today?

Chapter 26

SHIPHRA AND PUAH

"The king of Egypt said to the Hebrew midwives,
whose names were Shiphrah and Puah, 'When you
are helping the Hebrew women during childbirth on
the delivery stool, if you see that the baby is a boy, kill
him; but if it is a girl, let her live'" (Ex. 1:15–16).

Dear Shiphra and Puah,

You are amazing, God-fearing women. To do what you did, to defy the king the way you did takes courage. I don't know what you thought when you were called into the presence of the Egyptian king. I'm sure you were nervous. Anyone would have been. Did you have any idea what he was going to say to you? After all, because you were the midwives to the lowly women in the slave-labor pool, I would imagine that the king's summons came as a bit of a shock. Why on Earth would the king want to talk to you?

The two of you were kept busy delivering babies.

Scripture tells us the children of Israel were fruitful, and the land was filled with them. The fecundity of Hebrew women was rather alarming to the new king, who lamented that "the children of Israel are more and mightier than we Egyptians." He was prescient in his thinking. He could foresee that one day Israel would rebel, form an army, and destroy Egypt. I have to wonder how much rage must have been building in the Hebrew slaves against their taskmasters.

So the pharaoh of all Egypt summoned the two of you. His command was immediate and blunt: "Kill all the newborn males." I'm sure you bowed and said, "Yes, sir. Yes sir. We certainly will do that. No problem." But you both knew you would do no such thing.

You went back to your work delivering babies. Each newborn child was handed safely into a mother's arms, in direct disobedience of the king's command. Of course he heard about it. You were summoned yet again. The king was not happy. I have an idea that he raised his voice at you: "Didn't I order you to kill the boy babies? But you didn't do it, did you? Why did you defy my orders?"

But you both knew you would do no such thing.

Had you rehearsed what you would say if the king asked the question? I'm sure you both tried your utmost to look innocent, wide-eyed, and humble. You, Shiphra, crossed your fingers behind your back and said, "Oh, king, the Hebrew women have their boys before we even get to their bedsides. They are much livelier than the Egyptian women." And, Puah, you chimed in with, "That's right, sir. Try as we might, those baby boys are born before we arrive to help." (See Exodus 1:19.)

The king was not happy with you, but God was. I think you made God smile. The Ten Commandments had not yet been given, but lying was already understood to be unacceptable. I guess God was willing to make an exception in your case, even rewarding you two liars with houses of your own. And the Hebrews continued to multiply, so you still had plenty of work to do.

Shiphra, your name means "beauty." Puah, your name means "splendor." I suppose we all can agree that what the two of you did was a beautiful thing. You did it for love. And love, to borrow from a song popular in my country in the 1950s, is a many-splendored thing. (Not to spoil a happy ending, but Pharaoh promptly ordered all baby boys thrown into the river.)

S-o courageous were you.

H-aving faced an angry sovereign and

I-n danger of losing your own life,

P-utting truth aside, you

H-id your intentions, and thus you

R-adically changed all subsequent history.

A-ll hail to the life bringer.

P-lotting

U-nder difficult circumstances

A-nd crossing your fingers behind your back, you

H-ad the joy of saving many baby boys.

REFLECTING

1. Under what circumstances would you tell a lie?

2. What is the difference between a lie and a "white lie?"

3. Do you believe all good deeds are rewarded? How so?

4. How does God work in our lives to accomplish His purposes?

Chapter 27

SUSANNA

"Jesus traveled about from one town and village to another, proclaiming the good news of the kingdom of God. The Twelve were with him, and also some women who had been cured of evil spirits and diseases: Mary (called Magdalene) from whom seven demons had come out; Joanna the wife of Chuza, the manager of Herod's household; Susanna; and many others. These women were helping to support them out of their own means" (Luke 8:1–3).

Dear Susanna,

You are named in Scripture only once. Dr. Luke reported that Jesus healed you but did not mention the nature of your illness. Were you a leper who was isolated from society? Had you suffered from female complaints like the woman with the issue of blood? Did you limp? Could you stand? We'll never know. One thing we do know: Jesus is the Great Physician, and you sought Him for a miracle of healing. We know your healing took place in Galilee very early in the Master's ministry. And we know you joined "many other women" who, after being healed, became followers of the Lord.

When Luke wrote about the women who followed Jesus from Galilee, he wrote, almost as an afterthought, that you and other women supported the ministry out of your own resources. Bible readers in my day rarely stop to think that Jesus and His disciples had expenses. But they did. They had to eat. They needed clothes and sandals. They once rented an upper room. So it interests me that you women underwrote the endeavor. I assume you bought the groceries and did the cooking and kitchen cleanup. I hope you had the opportunity to share the Good News with other women you encountered in your travels.

Perhaps you possessed a rare combination of qualities: strength and courage for the journey and sweetness and beauty of character.

Susanna, you were never mentioned by name again in Scripture. If you were one of the "many other women" who followed Jesus from Galilee, you were in the company of the Lord early in His ministry and far beyond. And if you continued to follow, you might have been one of the women at the cross, at the tomb, and in the upper room who witnessed the birth of the church at Pentecost, too.

Your name means "lily." Lilies are beautiful flowers and have a sweet perfume. I can see that if you lived up to your name, you would have been both sweet and beautiful. But you were no fragile flower. You needed strength and endurance to walk all those miles across Galilee. And Christ followers in your day required courage. Perhaps you possessed a rare combination of qualities: strength and courage for the journey and sweetness and beauty of character.

S-weet girl, you

U-ndertook to follow Jesus with other women healed,

S-aved from illness,

A-nd trusting in His love,

N-othing deterred your resolve;

N-o one could dissuade you.

A-ll your heart was what you gave Him in payment for your healing.

Reflecting

1. When have you needed physical healing?

2. Do you consider all healing miraculous?

3. When did you decide to follow Jesus?

4. How do you express your faith?

5. How have you influenced another person? If so, how?

Chapter 28

TABITHA

"In Joppa there was a disciple named Tabitha (in Greek her name is Dorcas); she was always doing good and helping the poor" (Acts 9:36).

Dear Tabitha,

I wonder at the miracles performed by God and the prophets in the Old Testament, as well as those by Jesus and His disciples in the New Testament. When death comes to take a family member, I have witnessed the grief of those who are left to mourn their loss. I wish Jesus would walk through the door and bring back the loved one, alive and healthy, ready to take up life on earth again.

In our present day, these things just don't happen. And theologians have discussed why this is so for centuries. "Christ followers in the modern world don't have enough faith," say some. "Those miracles were only for that time and place, not for the present age," say others. I, for one, have no idea why you could be raised from the dead but my deceased relatives cannot. I'm glad the Apostle Peter was available to you.

Yours is a good story. You lived in Joppa. Luke, in his book about the early church, called you a disciple. You spent your days helping others: sewing for poor women and children and, no doubt, helping in other ways wherever you saw a need. There are people in the world who scramble to get rich, shoving people out of their way, intent on accumulating more and more. They care not for the poor. They are indifferent to the hungry. They do nothing to help the homeless. Not you, Tabitha. Whenever you saw a need, you helped to the best of your ability. I have often thought about what I would like people to say about me after I'm gone from this world. I have decided I want them to remember me and say, "She left it better than she found it." That could be said of you. In fact, it was said of you.

When you became sick and died, Peter was in Lydda, close to your city. The disciples sent two men *She left it* to fetch him. When they got back to your *better than* house in Joppa, Peter was taken upstairs *she found it.* to the room where your body lay. All the widows crowded around him, weeping and showing him garments you had sewed for them. He sent everyone out of the room and knelt at your bedside to pray. Suddenly, he said to you, "Tabitha, get up." And you did. You took Peter's hand, and he helped you stand. I can only imagine the joy and amazement the believers felt when Peter opened that bedroom door and called to them: "Here is Tabitha, alive and well!" I imagine pandemonium ensued.

You know, Tabitha, that if you had not been raised by the power of God, people would have mourned you and told all their friends how you had helped them by giving them clothes you had sewn. And, although you were raised once, you did die again one day. If I could have attended your memorial service, I would have stood when the preacher asked if anyone had anything to say about the deceased. And I would have said, with joy and gratitude at the memory of your life, "She left it better than she found it."

T-he widows of Joppa wept

A-t the news of your death

B-ecause of the loving help you gave. The

I-nfinite God,

T-aking notice of Peter's prayer, must have decided you

H-ad more work to do in Joppa.

A-lleluia!

REFLECTING

1. Do you believe in miracles? Have you ever seen or experienced one?

2. What positive qualities did Tabitha possess?

3. What do you want people to say about you after your death?

Chapter 29

VASHTI

"This is what happened during the time of Xerxes, the Xerxes who ruled over 127 provinces stretching from India to Cush. At that time King Xerxes reigned from his royal throne in the citadel of Susa, and in the third year of his reign he gave a banquet for all his nobles and officials. The military leaders of Persia and Media, the princes, and the nobles of the provinces were present" (Esther 1:1–3).

"On the seventh day, when King Xerxes was in high spirits from wine, he commanded the seven eunuchs who served him... to bring before him Queen Vashti, wearing her royal crown, in order to display her beauty to the people and nobles, for she was lovely to look at. But when the attendants delivered the king's command, Queen Vashti refused to come. Then the king became furious and burned with anger" (Esther 1:10–12).

Dear Vashti,

What an opulent life you led in the Persian palace! The descriptions of the lavish banquets, the elegant decor of the courtyards, the golden goblets—each one different from the others, the time consumed in entertainment, the number of slaves required to produce such a show, the beauty of the king's gardens, the vast wealth displayed: All this was breathtaking.

On the seventh day of a particularly elegant banquet, when your husband was full of wine and feeling expansive, he commanded that you come before the gathering of men at his banquet tables to impress his guests with your beauty.

This sounds suspiciously like every stag gathering since the beginning of time. I wonder if your husband wanted you to pop out of a cake, too? King Xerxes stipulated that you were to wear your crown. Rabbis have interpreted this to mean you were to wear your crown and nothing else. You, wise lady, sent your regrets, whereupon your husband, burning with anger, called in his advisors.

> *I wonder if your husband wanted you to pop out of a cake.*

The reaction of the advisors was predictable: "If the king's wife doesn't obey him, every woman in the kingdom will hear about it and will follow her example. And there will be nothing but disrespect and discord in the land. The kingdom will fall into chaos. Send out an edict that states that every man should be ruler over his own household." And that's what your husband did.

When the king's anger had cooled a bit, he thought about what he had done. Before he could decide what to do next, his closest attendants suggested a massive beauty contest to find the most beautiful girl in the kingdom to replace you. "We can bring in girls from all the provinces. We can give them beauty treatments and arrange for a coach to teach them how to please a man. Then the one who pleases the king can take the place of Vashti." Your husband agreed. How could he resist?

At this point, you disappear from the narrative. What did you do? Where did you go? How did you live? Was there some alimony in the arrangement, or were you dismissed at the door of the palace and told never to return? I suppose we'll never know.

We do know, however, several things about you: you did not accede to your husband's desire to show you off to a crowd of drunken men. You had a mind of your own, and you had a sense of decency that the king and his guests lacked. Also, you might have been the only woman in all of Scripture to refuse to obey a direct order from her husband. And in disobeying, your wish not to see him was granted—forever.

V-anity was not your motivation,

A-lthough a beauty you

S-urely were.

H-usbands and kings may command and

T-ake umbrage when refused.

I declare a stubborn wife both virtuous and triumphant.

REFLECTING

1. Do you think that husbands should expect their wives to obey commands? Why or why not?

2. What does Scripture mean when it says that husbands and wives should submit themselves to one another? (See Ephesians 5:21–24.)

3. Do you believe that men and women stand on level ground at the foot of the cross? What does that question mean to you?

Chapter 30

ZIPPORAH

"Now a priest of Midian had seven daughters, and they came to draw water and fill the troughs to water their father's flock. Some shepherds came along and drove them away, but Moses got up and came to their rescue and watered their flock... Moses agreed to stay with the man, who gave his daughter Zipporah to Moses in marriage" (Ex. 2:16–17, 21).

"At a lodging place on the way, the Lord met Moses and was about to kill him. But Zipporah took a flint knife, cut off her son's foreskin and touched Moses' feet with it. 'Surely you are a bridegroom of blood to me,' she said. So the Lord let him alone. (At that time she said 'bridegroom of blood,' referring to circumcision)" (Ex. 4:24–26).

Dear Zipporah,

Did you have any idea that the good-looking Egyptian who helped you and your sisters at the well was no

Egyptian at all, but a Hebrew on the lam? Did he ever tell you he had run away from Egypt after he killed an Egyptian who was beating a Hebrew slave? Moses certainly looked like an Egyptian—and with good reason. He grew up in the house of Pharaoh and was educated by the best teachers Egypt had to offer. He was accustomed to living well.

Scripture indicates that Moses was content to live in Midian in your father's house. Your father gave you to him in marriage, and Moses settled down for a long life of tending your father's flocks. When your baby boy was born, you named him Gershom. The name means "expulsion"—a reminder, perhaps, that Moses was persona non grata in Egypt.

One day, when Moses was tending your father's sheep near Mount Sinai, he got involved with God and a burning bush. Having a conversation with the Almighty is what most of us would term "extraordinary." That day, over Moses's many objections, God gave him explicit instructions to take the Hebrew slave population out of Egypt to a land flowing with milk and honey. God did mention that the new land was populated by Canaanites, Hittites, Amorites, Perizzites, Hivites, and Jebusites.

Not to worry. God promised to take care of any problems that might arise. When Moses got home, he told you to pack a bag. What was he thinking? What was your reaction? He sought your father's permission for a return trip to Egypt. With permission granted, Moses put you and your sons (by this time, you had another boy) on a donkey.

One night, you stopped at an inn. Scripture states, "The Lord met Moses and tried to kill him" (Ex. 4:24). Now, there is a sentence heavy with mystery! If God ordered your husband to lead the Hebrews out of slavery, why kill him? Surely this was no cosmic game God was playing. Why was God so angry at Moses? Scripture is not explicit, but it became apparent that Moses had not circumcised Gershom. Circumcision is the sign of Israel's covenant relationship with God. To neglect to circumcise a son meant that he was not a part of the covenant. You, Zipporah, took a flint, cut off your son's foreskin, and threw it at Moses's feet. You seemed a bit angry when you said, "You are a bloody husband to me." Now, what could that possibly mean? I had to do some research to find out.

They should have. You saved their brother's life.

One commentary stated that Moses was, no doubt, circumcised on the eighth day after his birth, but some cultures circumcised as a premarital rite, making the groom "a bloody husband." Your action symbolized Moses as being a bridegroom of blood. God's anger was appeased. All of this sounds strange indeed to people of my century.

After that, you disappear from the narrative, while Moses was kept busy for the next forty years. Did you go back to Midian, or did you follow Moses? Scripture records that his brother, Aaron, and his sister, Miriam, murmured against him because of you—the "Cushite woman"—he had married (Num. 12:1–2). They obviously did not hold you in high regard. They should have. You saved their brother's life. God allowed Moses to live only because of your intervention.

Z-ipporah,

I wonder what you thought when your

P-apa, the

P-riest of Midian,

O-ffered you in marriage to Moses.

R-eality set in. God's call came.

A-ll his life from that point on was not

H-is own, nor was it yours.

REFLECTING

1. What do you understand about God's calling?

2. How do you deal with the unexpected?

3. Do you believe God still calls people to do His work?

4. How does God equip and sustain those whom He calls?

AFTERWORD

A story keeps coming to my mind. It really happened. When we were missionaries in southern Brazil, a group of mission-minded folk from First Baptist Church in Amarillo, Texas, came to our town to lead an evangelistic effort.

The leader of the group was Morris Cobb. His wife, Wynona, was a part of that group, and I had the joy of being her translator that week. We had a wonderful time of fellowship. Morris and Wynona had dedicated themselves to doing this kind of work on a volunteer basis. I had the opportunity to hear some wonderful stories. She told me that a group had gone to Singapore and stayed in a large hotel. After breakfast the first morning, Morris said, "Lunch is at the hotel at noon. Speak to five people about the love of Jesus before then, or you don't get lunch." Everyone laughed but were not sure whether or not he was joking.

Two women from the group went to the mezzanine, where there were various shops. They entered a jewelry store. The owner greeted them. After a courteous greeting, he asked, "Who are you? Why are you in Singapore?"

They responded, "We are two little old ladies in tennis shoes. We have come to talk to people about Jesus."

He asked if they were with a group, and they said yes.

He said, "Bring your group here at six o'clock for supper."

"But there are forty of us," they responded.

"Come," he said. "Bring your group."

At the appointed hour, the group arrived. A banquet was waiting. After dinner, the man stood and said, "My name is Danny. Last night, I had a dream that someone would come today to tell me about eternal life. I am prepared to hear. I have washed my body with new soap. I have put on new clothes. I have given alms to the poor people in the street. Now, open your book and feed me."

Morris stood and opened his Bible to the account of Paul's sermon on Mars Hill. He began, "Oh, Danny, man of Singapore, I perceive that in all things you are very religious. I have walked the streets of your city, and I have seen the altars to your gods. I am here to proclaim to you the Unknown God. His name is Jesus."

All through that presentation, Danny was saying, "Yes, yes, yes."

This little book you hold in your hand is simple. It is based on a few Bible characters. I think we sometimes take the Bible for granted. Do we forget the power that exists in the Word? Are we so saturated with Bible knowledge that we treat Scripture as commonplace? Let us remember that the living Word of God is precious, holy, and powerful.

WORKS CITED

Allen, Clifton J., ed. The Broadman Bible Commentary. Nashville, TN: Broadman Press, 1971.

del Mastro, M. L. All the Women of the Bible. Edison, NJ: Castle Books, 2004.

Matthews, Victor H. Manners and Customs in the Bible. Peabody, MA: Hendrickson Publishers, 1991.

Moltmann-Wendel, Elisabeth. The Women Around Jesus. New York: Crossroad Publishing, 1997.

Meyers, Carol. Women in Scripture: A Dictionary of Named and Unnamed Women in the Hebrew Bible, the Apocryphal/Deuterocanonical Books, and the New Testament. New York: Houghton Mifflin, 2000.

Scofield, C. I., ed. "Dictionary of Scripture Proper Names" in The Scofield Reference Bible. New York: Oxford University Press, 1917, 162.

Stagg, Evelyn and Frank. Woman in the World of Jesus. Philadelphia: Westminster John Knox Press, 1978.

IF YOU'RE A FAN OF THIS BOOK, WILL YOU HELP ME SPREAD THE WORD?

www.robertadamon.me
There are several ways you can help me get the word out about the message of this book...

- Post a 5-Star review on Amazon.

- Write about the book on your Facebook, Twitter, Instagram – any social media you regularly use!

- If you blog, consider referencing the book, or publishing an excerpt from the book with a link back to my website. You have my permission to do this as long as you provide proper credit and backlinks.

- Recommend the book to friends – word-of-mouth is still the most effective form of advertising.

- Purchase additional copies to give away as gifts. You can do that by going to my website at: www.robertadamon.me

The best way to connect with me is at: www.robertadamon.me OR P.O. Box 3402, Chester, VA 23831

ENJOY THESE OTHER BOOKS BY ROBERTA DAMON

A Voice Beyond Weeping: A Memoir

Who you are is shaped by where you've been. Roberta Damon masterfully and poignantly takes you on a journey of discovery from her upbringing in the Depression-era dust plains of Oklahoma.

You will find yourself thoroughly engaged in the gripping telling of this story including the discovery of the third of the author's three mothers, her growth from infancy to significant adulthood set against the backdrop of faith and redemption.

Theirs is the Kingdom: A Fictionalized History of the Early Christian Church

Power – Politics – Romance – Intrigue – Faith
Roberta Damon skillfully blends historical facts and characters to create a masterful, inspiring and educational read!

Dear Mrs. Noah: Letters to Unnamed Women of the Bible

There are many Biblical women whose stories are known, but whose names are not recorded. Roberta Damon writes letters to 34 of these women, gives them appropriate names, and grants them new identity.

You can order these books from

 BARNES&NOBLE

or wherever you purchase your favorite books. You can also order these books from my website at: www.robertadamon.me

NEED A SPEAKER FOR YOUR NEXT PROGRAM?

Invite me to speak to your group or ministry. I have forty years of public speaking experience. If you would like to have me come speak to your group or at an upcoming event, please contact me at: www.robertadamon.me OR P.O. Box 3402, Chester, VA 23831

COMMENTS FROM PARTICIPANTS:

"A breath of fresh air."
"I could listen to her all day."
"Come back again. We loved hearing you."
"I loved your story."

POSSIBLE TOPICS

- Women in the Bible
- Marriage and Family
- Grief
- Depression
- Identity Issues
- Family of Origin--including my own story